Jan Krämer, Stefan Seifert (eds.)

Communications Regulation in the Age of Digital Convergence

Legal and Economic Perspectives

Communications Regulation in the Age of Digital Convergence

Legal and Economic Perspectives

Jan Krämer
Stefan Seifert
(eds.)

universitätsverlag karlsruhe

Impressum

Universitätsverlag Karlsruhe
c/o Universitätsbibliothek
Straße am Forum 2
D-76131 Karlsruhe
www.uvka.de

Universitätsverlag Karlsruhe 2009
Print on Demand

ISBN: 978-3-86644-387-7

Preface

These proceedings comprise the contributions to the "International Workshop on Communications Regulation in the Age of Digital Convergence: Legal and Economic Perspectives", which was held in Karlsruhe, Germany on December 2, 2008.

The workshop was sponsored by the KIT, the merger of the Universität Karlsruhe (TH) and the Forschungszentrum Karlsruhe, within its Competence Area "Technology, Culture and Society"—one of the six newly founded Competence Areas that constitute the umbrella over all research activities within the KIT. Traditionally, the University of Karlsruhe has been a technical university with a strong background in engineering and the natural sciences—and the same holds for the Forschungszentrum Karlsruhe. In 1886 Heinrich Hertz discovered electromagnetic waves at the University of Karlsruhe and was the first to transfer waves from a sender to a receiver. About 100 years later, the first e-mail in Germany was received at the University of Karlsruhe. With its physics, electrical engineering, information technology, and computer science departments (among others), the University of Karlsruhe is continuing this tradition today. However, it also acknowledges the importance and the responsibility of linking the university's technical research activities with cultural and social issues. In this light, the Competence Area "Technology, Culture and Society" was established under the special mentoring of the university's President's Office. Having laid the foundations for radio telegraphy, it is also logical to investigate business opportunities that are based on wireless communication and to explore how regulatory bodies can best facilitate both innovation and competition so that society can make the best use of communication technology.

The "International Workshop on Communications Regulation in the Age of Digital Convergence" brought together lawyers and economists from both academia and industry to discuss current topics in telecommunications regulation. The changes driven by the digitalization and convergence of networks and devices will have a significant impact on society and culture as well as economic growth and wealth. From the *business perspective,* appropriate incentives for investments in innovative products and services are crucial. From the *consumer perspective*, the regulator must provide a level playing field for competition between communications service providers so that the forces of the market will ensure the most useful products and services at the lowest costs. And finally, the *social perspective* calls for approaches that allow fair access to media and communications services. It is alarming that in Germany almost one million households have no access to broadband Internet because broadband is not provided in rural areas—by this measure Germany ranks among the least developed countries in Europe.

The workshop was co-organized by the *Institute of Information Systems and Management (IISM)* and the *Shared Research Group Industrial Organization in Telecommunications Markets*. This research group was established within the Excellence Initiative of the German federal and state governments and over the course of the foundation of the KIT. It is part of the "Communications & Behavior" department of the chair "Information & Market Engineering" headed by Professor Dr. Christof Weinhardt at the Institute of Information Systems and Management. The research group deals with questions concerning business strategies and regulation in networked-based industries such as energy, traffic, and especially telecommunications by looking at them from a micro-economic perspective. It applies theoretical—particularly game theoretical—models, empirical studies, and laboratory experiments in order to investigate the effects of regulatory interventions and to develop viable policies for regulatory frameworks that facilitate economic efficiency and encourage innovation. Moreover, the group analyzes promising business opportunities and strategies in an ever-changing environment.

The positive feedback we received in the run-up to this workshop underscores the importance of these topics and the immense interest from both academics and industry representatives. Furthermore, never before have we received so many comments about how important a workshop is. This enthusiasm encouraged us to collect the contributions of the presenters and to compile them in these proceedings. We are very proud to have been able to attract such a stellar set of highly reputed experts in the field of telecommunications to contribute to this volume; they hail from academia, regulatory offices, and industry. More than that, we are very grateful for the time and effort the contributors put into their presentations at the first KIT Workshop on Communications Regulation; their contributions are printed in these proceedings.

This volume covers a great deal of the relevant regulatory topics with respect to the convergence phenomenon. The contributions highlight the fact that the technical advancements and regulatory changes in the telecommunications industry have had a tremendous economic impact and have in turn posed new regulatory challenges. However, the speakers at the workshop also stressed the fact that none of the regulatory challenges is impossible to overcome.

Sometimes, as can be seen in Jürgen Kühling's contribution, only small legislative adjustments are necessary in order to accommodate the challenges. Sometimes more substantial decisions on the role of future sector-specific regulation in the telecommunications sector have to be made. This is very explicitly illustrated in Iris Henseler-Unger's contribution. Sometimes the different stakeholders have radically different views on the same topic. The discussion on the digital dividend is a case in point: It illustrates the broad "spectrum" of proposals, ranging from dedicated allocation through auctions, as put forward here in the article by Peter Cramton, to open and laissez-faire usage, as illustrated by Simon Forge's contribution. In any case, mobile operators, such as Vodafone, demand regulatory stability upon which they can base their investment decisions.

Certainly, more research is needed in order to ensure that future regulatory decisions are made on sound ground. We hope that the workshop and this volume will inspire continuing research in this area.

Karlsruhe, January 2009

Jan Krämer
Stefan Seifert

Contents

Contributors

Prof. Peter Cramton, Ph.D.
Department of Economics, University of Maryland, USA

Simon Forge, Ph.D.
SCF Associates Ltd, UK

Dr. Iris Henseler-Unger
Bundesnetzagentur, Germany

Dr. Stephan Korehnke
Vodafone D2 GmbH, Germany

Dr. Jan Krämer
Institute of Information Systems and Management, Universität Karlsruhe (TH), Germany
Industrial Organisation in Telecommunications Markets, Karlsruhe Institute of Technology

Prof. Dr. Jürgen Kühling, LL.M.
Institut für Immobilienrecht, Universität Regensburg, Germany

Jun.-Prof. Dr. Stefan Seifert
Institute of Information Systems and Management, Universität Karlsruhe (TH), Germany
Industrial Organisation in Telecommunications Markets, Karlsruhe Institute of Technology

Prof. Dr. Indra Spiecker genannt Döhmann, LL.M. (Georgetown University)
Institut für Informations- und Wirtschaftsrecht, Universität Karlsruhe (TH), Germany

Prof. Dr. Ingo Vogelsang
Department of Economics, Boston University, USA

Introduction

Jan Krämer, Stefan Seifert

The communications industry is one of the biggest engines of economic growth, and following the liberalization of the sector in the late twentieth century, it has undergone a tremendous transformation. Moreover, the ongoing digitalization of infrastructure and services is currently driving the development of the communications sector, particularly with respect to new economic prospects and regulatory challenges. Due to the phenomenon of *digital convergence*, companies employing distinct telecommunications technologies can offer virtually the same services and have thereby become competitors. A major challenge of the current regulatory effort is therefore to establish and maintain a technology-neutral regulatory framework that will ensure a level playing field for all competitors. However, in Europe and the US, many legacies of the analog age have remained unchanged and continue to be a source of technology-dependent regulation.

These proceedings are divided among three parts, each dealing with different facets of the convergence and digitalization phenomena.

Part 1 deals with *Convergence & Neutrality* and the contributors in this part look at the different types of "neutrality" that have to be considered in converging communications markets.

First, *Jürgen Kühling* comments on technological neutrality. Technological neutrality is one of the key concepts underpinning the new regulatory framework for electronic communications networks and services in the European Union. In essence, technological neutrality seeks to ensure regulatory even-handedness for relatively homogenous services that are provided in a single market, but use alternative technologies or platforms for delivery. In his article, Jürgen Kühling points out some examples where current regulatory practice violates the principle of technological neutrality.

Jürgen Kühling is a law professor, formerly at the University of Karlsruhe, and since 2007 at the University of Regensburg. He is well known for his research on the regulation of network industries and also serves on the editorial board of several academic journals in this area.

Ingo Vogelsang addresses the issue of network neutrality. While technological neutrality refers to neutrality towards different types of delivery platforms, network neutrality deals with neutrality towards different types of traffic on a given delivery platform. In particular, network neutrality addresses the issue of Internet service providers' traffic shaping, i.e. the prioritization or degradation of certain types of traffic, such as VoIP or file-sharing protocols. The network neutrality debate started in the United States when the Federal Communications Commission (FCC) changed the classification of Internet transmission from the category of "telecommunications services" to that of "information services", whereby Internet service providers were no longer subject to non-discrimination restrictions of their services. According to classic economic rationale, ISPs then have an incentive to charge content providers premium prices for preferential access to broadband transmission services. Finally, in October 2007, it was reported that Comcast (the largest US cable operator and No. 2 Internet provider) had been engaging in traffic shaping by hindering peer-to-peer filesharing traffic. Advocates of network neutrality, academics and practitioners alike, see traffic shaping as a threat to the Internet's function as an innovation enabler. In his article, Ingo Vogelsang shows that the network neutrality debate concerns not only the US, but has important ramifications for Europe as well.

Ingo Vogelsang is a professor of economics at Boston University and an internationally respected industrial organization and policy expert specializing in public utility regulation and particularly telecommunications economics. Originating from Germany, where he received his doctorate degree in economics, and having worked in Boston for more than twenty years, Ingo Vogelsang is certainly also an expert on supranational regulatory issues.

Finally, the contribution by *Indra Spiecker gen. Döhmann* deals with economic neutrality in terms of regulatory intervention. In this context, economic neutrality means that the intervention of the regulator is supposed to ensure efficient competition, but should not undermine basic economic incentives. Indra Spiecker stresses this very regulatory conundrum: On the one hand, regulation requires knowledge of business-critical information (especially of that pertaining to former monopolists). For instance, in order to effect price regulation, the regulator must know the long-run marginal costs of the incumbent, which is business-critical information. Normally, the confidentiality of this information is protected by law. However, on the other hand, the regulator must at least partially reveal this information in order to justify its actions to the competitors. Of course, the revelation of business-critical information severely impedes the innovation incentives of the firms and is thus not an economically neutral act.

Indra Spiecker gen. Döhmann is a law professor at the University of Karlsruhe and the University of Freiburg. Her main research areas are information society law, protection of information and behavioral law and economics.

The second part of these proceedings is dedicated to *Convergence & Digital Dividend*. The term digital dividend reflects the fact that digital signal transmission needs much less spectrum than traditional analog transmission, and hence can be said to yield a "dividend". Currently, almost half of the electromagnetic spectrum that is suited for both in-house and long-distance coverage—about 400 MHz in total—is used for broadcasting services. When analog is switched to digital, only 10% to 25% of this spectrum is necessary to transmit about the same number of channels in roughly the same quality. The remaining spectrum is referred to as the digital dividend. It could be used for example by the radio stations to improve audio and video quality or to increase the number of TV channels. Alternatively, the spectrum could be used for mobile services or broadband Internet services in rural areas. However, the boundaries between the different uses are often blurred due to the phenomenon of digital convergence, whereby e.g. mobile handheld devices can also be used to receive TV signals.

Peter Cramton recommends allowing the market to decide what the best use of the spectrum is. Thus, he suggests auctioning off the digital dividend, because auctioning would ostensibly result in the assignation of the spectrum to those who value it most. In particular, he proposes a package clock auction with closest-to-Vickrey core pricing, an auction format that not only facilitates substitution and price discovery, but also induces truthful bidding.

Peter Cramton is a professor of economics at the University of Maryland. He is an outstanding expert in auction theory and practice. The main focus of his research is the design of multi-item auctions for particular real-world situations.

Stephan Korehnke lays out the position of a mobile operator with respect to the provision of broadband Internet access. He explains that a significant share of the digital dividend will be necessary to cover rural areas with an appropriate bandwidth and thus claims that operators will be allowed to pool spectrum in these areas in order to enhance technical efficiency and reduce the costs of the network.

Stephan Korehnke is a lawyer with Vodafone Germany holds a doctoral degree in law from the University of Cologne. He is the head of the Department for Regulatory Affairs and heavily involved in Vodafone's current activities with respect to the allocation of additional spectrum, including the digital dividend.

Simon Forge presents a very different approach to using the dividend. Basically, he argues against issuing exclusive individual licenses. Rather, the spectrum should be used collectively on a commons basis. This approach would allow for more efficient use and create additional incentives for innovation.

Simon Forge is an engineer with more than twenty years of experience in the information industries. He is the director of SCF associates and mainly works on strategy formulation, marketing, and business planning.

The third part is dedicated to *Convergence & Innovation.* The long-run goal of regulation is to establish efficient and enduring competition in the telecommunications industry. Creating long-run incentives for innovation and thereby effective and efficient competition is one of the key objectives of regulatory offices in Germany and abroad. Efficient competition also results in an economic environment that fosters the firms' incentives to innovate and invest in new infrastructure and services. However, academics, regulators, and practitioners have not yet managed to reach a consensus on which regulatory regime would generally be the most effective in promoting innovation. As a first step, access-based regulation has proven to be a successful means of establishing competition in the sector. According to the ladder of investment theory (which was put forth by Martin Cave and Ingo Vogelsang), access-based competition facilitates entry into the telecommunications market for new firms, which would otherwise be stymied by high investment costs and the remaining monopolistic bottleneck of the local loop. In the long run, these firms are then expected to use their profits from access-based competition to invest in their own infrastructures and eventually become facilities-based competitors. Facilities-based competition—and there is general agreement on this issue—is the most desirable form if competition because it tends to be enduring.

In the final contribution of the proceedings, *Iris Henseler-Unger* takes the view of the regulator and shows the difficulties that the regulatory offices face when they embark upon the assessment of different—and even contradictory—academic studies analyzing the suitability of prospective regulatory regimes with respect to innovation incentives.

Iris Henseler-Unger is vice president of the German regulatory authority, the Federal Network Agency (Bundesnetzagentur), and thus a member of the executive board of the German regulatory body, which presides over the Department of Economic Questions of Telecommunication Regulation and others. Iris Henseler-Unger holds a doctoral degree in economics from the University of Mannheim and is therefore in a perfect position to evaluate both the economic and regulatory viewpoints.

Part 1: Convergence & Neutrality

Convergence and Regulatory Challenges at National and Supranational Level

Jürgen Kühling

1. Introduction

There are several reasons particularly for me to come to this conference. First, I think it is a very important and very interesting issue that we will talk about today and the first sessions show the various aspects of this complex topic. Second, it is very important to discuss those issues from both an economic and a legal perspective. And Karlsruhe is a very good place to work with an interdisciplinary approach on that subject. Third, it is always nice to come back to Karlsruhe, where my career as a professor started in 2004.

It is also nice that I can start with the opening presentation. Even though it is a very complex topic, I hope to be able to give a sort of framework for today's discussions. To do this I will try to give a full picture of the debate from a legal perspective. If you look at the developments on the market relating to IPTV, Handy TV, triple play, and quadruple play, one might think that our regulatory framework for information society might not be suitable for all those developments ahead of us. Particularly in the media sector, a lot of people say we need to make a radical change to our framework. Within the next thirty minutes I will analyze whether such a radical change is really necessary or what kind of changes we need instead.

2. Structure of the Presentation

I will present my ideas in four steps. My first step will be a short introduction. What kind of convergence processes are we facing? Technological convergence, convergence at the content level, and supply-side convergence are the three main types of convergence phenomena, which I will explain. My second step will focus on the structure of our regulatory framework and I will try to show that its basic structure is well suited to face the changes we are expecting. The most important regulatory principle is technological neutrality. Moreover, in Germany we have a specific approach with a sharp regulatory differentiation at the content level which you could call a principle of "separate and regulate", meaning that you split up the services and regulate them according to different models. But there are still some remaining challenges and this will be my third point. What kind of challenges remain and what kind of changes do we need in our regulatory structure? Finally, I will try to sum up my ideas in a conclusion.

3. The Different Types of Convergence Phenomena

First, you have to sharply differentiate on an analytical level between the three different types of convergence phenomena. The basis of all those convergence processes is technological convergence. We have various platforms that can offer identical services. You can't say what kind of service you are facing, only looking at the infrastructure as it was five years ago. You looked at the cable and you knew that it was television that came through the cable. You looked at the plain old telephone system and you knew it was telephony we were talking about. This paradigm is obsolete now, and of course the overall process of convergence has been revolutionized by the advent of IP, meaning that everything is mastered by Internet protocol and all networks and services are able to work together. This makes all those other convergence processes we are seeing possible. Thus, the services are not linked to a specific infrastructure anymore, and this makes it more complicated for the regulatory authorities to identify what kind of service is at hand in order to apply the appropriate regulatory system. But what is even more challenging is the convergence process at the content level. Here we are facing massive changes in consumer preferences. If you particularly look at surveys analyzing what kind of media young people are consuming, the statistics show a distinct gap between young and older people. You can see that young people are using the Internet, making extensive use of the information channels and watching YouTube rather than classic television. This will have implications for the regulatory model, particularly at the constitutional level. I will come back to this particular issue at the end of my presentation. Moreover, there is another important development: The roles of the providers and the receivers are becoming blurred. In this sense, we have what you can call "prosumants"—a hybrid of producer and consumer. YouTube once again is the best example to show that it's not like it used to be, with a producer of content on the one side and the multipoint audience on the other. Again, this will have strong implications for the regulatory approach. Finally, we have other small changes which raise the question of whether we can still apply for example the broadcasting model to broadcasting content, such as teleshopping. Of course, that doesn't make much sense and that's why the Rundfunkstaatsvertrag (German Broadcasting Act) has been changed to offer a different regulatory model for teleshopping.

Thus, we have all those convergence processes and developments at the content level calling for modifications of the regulatory model with its sharp distinction between the different types of content in Germany and also in most of the other European countries. And of course all those convergence processes raise the question of whether classical television is still valid—as the German Constitutional Court just a hundred meters away from here claims—as the guiding medium for the model. This has massive implications for the discussion on the digital dividend, which will be discussed in the afternoon. Therefore, at the content level, we have convergence processes that are also related to each other. We have convergence tendencies at the supply side. We have cross-market entries and vertical integration processes like triple play, quadruple play, Handy TV, etc. This process of vertical integration is of particular interest. Former Telecom undertakings are entering the VDSL television distribution markets and vice versa. The cable distributors are entering the telephony market. That is all familiar and called triple play. Moreover, those telecommunication providers are trying to move into the content markets. They are already into the telemedia markets and they are also trying to get into the television market. Handy TV is a good example of various market players trying to move into their competitors' markets. For example, publishers have finally obtained the license for Handy TV from the media regulatory authorities at the state level (Landesmedienanstalten). Thus, publishers, both offline and telemedia, are trying to move into the TV distribution and production markets. Traditional broadcasters have also tried to get into this market. Moreover, mobile electronic communication providers are trying to get into the Handy TV market. This will have important implications for the definition of markets in the long run. You can easily follow all the discussions we are having about this in Germany and also in Great Britain at the moment. We are discussing to what extent public broadcasters should be allowed to penetrate the telemedia market. And just a week ago, BBC, which tried to get into the telemedia market with a number of specific offers, was barred from using public money, the fees, to get into those markets. This is a result of the European Commission's three step test, which is also applied to German public broadcasters on the basis of EC State Aid Control.

At the end of the day, the question in my mind is not so much if public *broadcasters* should be allowed to move into the telemedia markets, but rather if we should apply the public broadcasting *model* to the telemedia markets too. In other words, do we have any market failures that make it necessary to have a specific production process? And this is the question raised by the three step test, the public value test, of the European Commission.

From an economic point of view, this test can help to determine if there is really a market failure, which can help us decide if it is necessary to have this convergence and to apply the public broadcasting model to telemedia.

4. Principle of Technological Neutrality

With respect to technological neutrality, I believe it's a very smart principle. It comes from the European Telecommunication Law and in my opinion it solves most of the problems we have in relation to technological convergence. In other words, technological neutrality is the answer to technological convergence. It simply says that all technical infrastructures have to be regulated in the same way. And it is important to note that this concept does not only mean that the infrastructure itself is regulated in the same way: It also means that regardless of the content you are distributing via those various infrastructures, the regulatory model will be the same. This is different, for example, in the United States, where the full broadcasting model is only applied to terrestrial distribution of broadcasting content. It is not applied to cable TV, and as far as I know, it's not applied to satellite TV either. The situation is different in Europe. I believe it is more convincing to have technological neutrality, because it guarantees a level playing field. Of course, the various types of infrastructures have to be regulated in a different manner to some extent, because we have some types of infrastructures with shortages. Handy TV is one of those cases, because only one frequency with only one license was distributed. As a consequence, we had a scarcity problem, which was not the case for example in the distribution of television via the Internet. This may mean that the application of a consistent regulatory framework will have a different regulatory result. Nevertheless, technological neutrality guarantees that we will have a similar and level playing field for all of the different technological infrastructures.

5. Sharp Differences in Content Regulation

The second important regulatory principle in Germany stipulates that we have sharp regulatory differences at the content level. This is particularly the case with respect to the basic aim of broadcasting regulation, i.e. the aim of preserving pluralism. There is in particular a sharp distinction between broadcasting regulation on the one hand and telemedia regulation on the other. With respect to broadcasting regulation, we have a license model and a detailed regulation to safeguard pluralism. We have privileges for public broadcasting, particularly regarding access to fees and frequencies, and we have a special organization of these public broadcasting stations. None of this exists with respect to telemedia services; here we are applying a model of light-handed regulation. And of course once you have such sharp distinctions, the category to which your content belongs is very important. If it is public broadcasting, you have a completely different regulatory model than in telemedia regulation. And this makes it necessary to separate these various contents clearly. Moreover, it raises the question of whether we should continue to separate the various forms of content and regulate them in such a sharp and distinct way. In order to answer this question we have to distinguish between the various services. There are a lot of convergence processes that do not cause any problems at all, e.g. triple play, quadruple play. Those services are all related to the telecom markets and thus there is no danger of mixing up the various regulatory models. There is also no problem whatsoever in cases like Internet service providers moving into the content market. You just separate those services and apply different regulatory models. If for example Deutsche Telekom AG were to use its rights to transmit the Deutsche Fußballbundesliga [German National Soccer League] games and produce its own broadcasting program, the German Broadcasting Act would be applied to this service and it would be easy to separate those services and apply the broadcasting model. But Deutsche Telekom AG did not get into the broadcasting market itself, because it could not even ask for a license: As a company that is partially owned by the state, it cannot be granted a license because doing so would breach the principle of independence of broadcasters from state entities. Thus, this type of convergence does not question the model of "separate and regulate differently". Also, with respect to frequencies, we have no problems with the current model. If we take the case of Handy TV, the frequency for electronic communication services was granted to T-Systems by the Bundesnetzagentur [Federal Network Agency]. The TV license was allocated by the Landesmedienanstalten [State Media Broadcasting Authority]. Some people claim that it is due to convergence processes that it took so long to make those decisions. I think it's not a problem of convergence but a problem of the federal system that we are facing at the moment. Maybe the Bundesnetzagentur could have decided a bit quicker, but the bigger problem was the decision of the Landesmedienanstalten. And if it is true what I heard, that one million sheets of paper had to be carried through Germany from one Landesmedienanstalt to the next in order to arrive at a decision on which company would obtain the license, it shows the problems and costs of federalism in that context. And you know the end of the story: It took so long to make a decision that at the end of the day, "mobile 3.0", having received the license, declared that it had to stop its business four weeks ago. Now the license has to be allocated once again. But meanwhile we have at least changed the German Broadcasting Act. Now there is a rule according to which we will have a faster decision in such cases made by one central entity of the Landesmedienanstalten, and I guess if there is still somebody interested in going into the Handy TV market, the decision on the allocation of the license will be made quite a bit faster this time. Thus, it is not a problem of convergence, but a problem of federalism, which has some downsides. However, these problems can be solved quite easily and have been solved already—maybe too late for the Handy TV market, but at least fast enough for future markets. Taking this into account, I think it's convincing to stick to this model even if we should introduce some institutional changes, which I referred to with respect to the Landesmedienanstalten. The basic model, with transmission regulation in the Telecommunication Act, a content regulation with a sharp distinction between broadcasting and telemedia services, can be maintained. Of course there will be debates once we have new services: Which box do they fit into? But I think the model itself is quite convincing.

6. Remaining Challenges

Finally, what challenges remain? One important point we are discussing at the moment is whether our separation between those two boxes (telemedia and broadcasting) should work according to the idea of the impact on public opinion. Once a service has a heavy impact on public opinion, it belongs in the broadcasting box; otherwise, it would go in the telemedia box. This is the concept that was developed a hundred meters away by the German Constitutional Court (Bundesverfassungsgericht), and that's the basic distinction we have so far. But nowadays we are facing the problem that once you apply an importance model, a service such as Google may fall under the German Broadcasting Act. The importance of search results on content provided for by search engines is much higher with respect to forming public opinion than the relevance of a teleshopping channel or crime series on television. If you are not on the first or the second page of Google's search results, your content is not really present on the Internet. As a consequence, placement has a high relevance for forming public opinion. It's not surprising that the Landesmedienanstalten told us that in the future they may consider Google as a broadcaster and put it in the broadcasting box. The problem is that our broadcasting regulations are not designed for an entity such as Google. Just to take the example of safeguarding pluralism: If you look at how Google produces its search results, I would be delighted to see if the regulatory authority can put some kind of pluralism algorithm into this mechanism in order to introduce a degree of pluralism into a search engine. Our model of safeguarding pluralism doesn't work here. Thus, the German Broadcasting Act has to be adapted, including the definition of broadcasting. The German Broadcasting Act is under review at the moment anyway in order to adopt the model of the European Community, which distinguishes between linear and non-linear services. Linear services are services that are received simultaneously like classic TV. Thus, only classic TV will be kept in the heavy regulation box. I think this is the correct answer at the moment. As long as we do not have any suitable regulatory model for entities such as YouTube or Google, it's not a good idea to put them in the classic television box. Thus, they have to be kept in the telemedia box and we have to start thinking about whether we need any particular regulation for Google. At the moment, a model of self-regulation is being applied, and it works pretty well. But if you listen to public broadcasting lawyers, they want to spread the public broadcasting model. Even the University of Karlsruhe was participating in this trial to build a public search engine. I'm very sceptical about this approach and I'm also very sceptical as to whether smart public regulation of search engines is possible. To take just one example, if you think about the subject of manipulation from outside, Google is in a much better situation to adapt its system than any kind of public authority. As a consequence, self-regulation is working quite well at the moment, and I can't see any regulatory problem. Thus, it makes sense to put Google in the telemedia box. But we have to adjust our German Broadcasting Act to safeguard this solution.

What is very interesting at the moment, from both a legal and an economic point of view, is the discussion about applying the public broadcasting model to Internet content. There is a lot of bad economics in the market at the moment, with some saying that we have market failures everywhere, including in the online markets. For example, some argue that we have the same problems as in the public broadcasting area: It is very expensive to produce content, we have a high concentration, etc. None of that is true for online content. Online content and the Internet is the prototype of a pluralistic medium and I can't see any market failures for which we need any regulation or for which we need a public broadcasting model. This is particularly evident if you think about Anderson's articles, which explain that long tail markets are typical for the Internet. This will lead to much more pluralism in online markets as compared to broadcasting markets. Even the smallest demand will be satisfied in the Internet markets. As a consequence, there is no reason to spread the public broadcasting model to online markets. Nevertheless, there is a debate going on about it in Germany at the moment.

And again, the German Constitutional Court in Karlsruhe might be the place where a decision will be made on that issue. In other member states of the European Union, constitutional legal doctrine does not have as much influence on the development of the markets. In Germany we have a lot of lawyers saying that we need to spread the public broadcasting model to the Internet, referring to the constitutional legal doctrine. And it's true: Our constitutional legal doctrine is pretty much focused on classic television and implies that classic television is the guiding media. Classic television has to be protected and guarded, and this has consequences for example for the discussion on the allocation of the digital dividend. If you think that public broadcasting is that important from a constitutional point of view, you tend to decide that this third infrastructure, the terrestrial distribution infrastructure, has to be reserved to a large extent for public broadcasting, e.g. for high definition television or the transmission of more channels via the terrestrial infrastructure. But if you assume—again, also from a constitutional point of view—that other media are equally important, then the opposite view arises. I think, as we already have cable and satellite transmission of television, we don't need the terrestrial infrastructure as a third means of transmission, which is only used by 5% of our population anyway. On the contrary, it's quite evident that we instead need those frequencies for mobile transmissions in order to solve the problem of digital divide, which is still quite a problem in Germany. Thus, it's time for a change of constitutional concepts and it is a pity that the German Constitutional Court is still stuck on the old model, i.e. that classic television is the guiding media and that we need heavy regulation here.

7. Conclusion

To sum up, there is no reason for radical changes to the regulatory framework of information society in times of convergence. The basic construction of the German model and also to some extent of the European model, with its different regulatory concepts on the vertical and horizontal levels, is quite suitable with respect to all those various convergence processes. We instead need small but decisive modifications. It is very important to reduce the reach of broadcasting regulation and avoid a spill-over from heavy-handed regulation to light-handed regulation. And as I said, the three step test of the European Commission is a step towards that goal. It explicitly asks if there is a public value produced by the public broadcasters once they move into the online markets. It is a good test in terms of trying to avoid the spread of the public broadcasting model to the Internet. Finally, I think that due to cross-market entries, the market definitions will change and we will have more competition in the future on all information markets and particularly on infrastructure markets.

Convergence and Net Neutrality

Ingo Vogelsang

1. Introduction

As an economist I'm squeezed here between two lawyers, but certainly feel very comfortable, because I have already collaborated with Jürgen Kühling on several occasions. Our most recent collaboration consisted of two lawyers and two economists doing joint work on six papers and we are still talking with each other. Stefan Seifert's earlier remarks about Heinrich Hertz and the University of Karlsruhe reminded me of the connection between my university, Boston University, and Alexander Graham Bell. It's not actually a very good story, because Alexander Graham Bell was a professor at Boston University at the time he invented the telephone. After he resigned to concentrate his attention on the telephone invention, Boston University claimed that he invented the phone on BU time, implying that they should be entitled to the patent royalties. That dispute ended in a disaster for BU. As of today the small size of BU's endowment still reflects that fact.

So now let me turn to my main topic which is *convergence* and *net neutrality*. These are two of the big catch words of the digital age. In a sense convergence has been a progressive notion for a long time and still is. We are still looking forward towards convergence, although a lot of it has already happened by now. In contrast, net neutrality is more of a backward-looking concept, reflecting the internet's golden age, when all bits were treated equally. So we are combining two of these most important topics in one. At first glance net neutrality appears to be an American issue. It has been very prominent in the debate and there have been several proposals for net neutrality laws. But I want to argue that net neutrality is predominantly an issue of convergence that concerns all of us. So my talk will start in Section 2 with characterizing net neutrality and convergence and then, in Section 3, will highlight some specific features of net neutrality, such as quality of service, pricing and the role of content providers. Section 4 will emphasize competition, which is at the center of convergence and net neutrality. I will finish with some policy conclusions.

2. Characterization of Net Neutrality and Convergence

Net neutrality has many definitions, the original view being that it concerns discrimination against content and service providers. Only to a limited extent is it about discrimination against users. The extreme view has been that networks and ISPs should treat all bits equally independent of content, origin, destination, platform or type of service. This view is somewhat outdated now, although it's still comes up in all the debates. However, the more moderate view seems to prevail, which is that net neutrality violations or discrimination are not based on objective criteria and are inconsistent with efficient competition. The main examples of net neutrality violations are (1) blocking of content and service providers or (2) anti-competitive quality classifications and (3) price discrimination against or in favour of content or service providers. The original internet was viewed as being largely free of net neutrality violations, whereas one can argue that the public switched telephone network (PSTN) and cable TV have known discrimination all along.

So what is convergence? I don't want to go deeply into that, but just refer to Jürgen Kühling's presentation, where he has characterized two types of convergence: technological convergence and content convergence. I am restricting myself here largely to technological convergence, which means that the networks converge in such a way that each one of them provides all types of services and this is associated with all-IP networks and broadband access. To illustrate, let us consider three idealised types of service network combinations. (1) The old PSTN, which was associated with telephony, would have to accommodate the internet and TV in order to be converging. (2) The cable TV has to accommodate internet and telephone and (3) the internet has to accommodate telephone and TV. In addition, a number of new services are emerging or have emerged that are common to all these networks. The US has achieved partial convergence in the PSTN and the wireless network. It is quite incomplete in the sense that these networks still have a hard time providing TV services. They have very low video penetration and limited broadband penetration so that, outside metropolitan areas, they cannot provide all the services that we associate with convergence. The cable TV networks in the US are further along in this way; both in term of the technical ability to provide all the services, so that they can easily provide triple play. Also, there is much larger take up of telephony through cable TV networks than take up of video by the telephone networks. If you look at the internet, well that's not really an infrastructure in itself, so it is a little different. We have in the past associated the internet with the backbone networks. When it comes to the all-important access network the Internet is, however, actually part of the other two networks.

3. Specific Features of Net Neutrality

3.1 Quality of Service

So now let me turn to quality of service. The main point of convergence is that it makes all these networks grow together. So each network must be able to accommodate all the quality-of-service requirements that were associated with different networks before. Before convergence the PSTN was specialized in the service requirements of telephony and so was the wireless service. In particular, this means low tolerance for latency and jitter, but at the same time low capacity requirements. The cable TV networks had high capacity requirements and had to be able to provide uninterrupted TV service, which required adherence to a certain quality standard. Only the internet was offering best effort service and had fairly low latency requirements. But at the same time the capacity requirements for Internet services could vary immensely.

When the convergence actually occurs, each network has to accommodate the quality requirements of all these services. That means essentially three possibilities: One possibility is that the quality of service of all the networks is raised so that the requirements of all services are met at the same time. Essentially the capacity has to be expanded to such an extent that telephony can work uninterrupted and that further requirements of security etc. are met. All of that would have to be within the technical capabilities of these networks. It is precisely the aim of next generation networks (NGN) to achieve this kind of quality. It would be consistent with net neutrality. The other extreme possibility is to actually lower the quality-of-service requirements of some of the services. So, one would have to live essentially with the Voice-over-the-Internet-Protocol (VoIP) kind of model based on the best effort internet. That would also be compatible with net neutrality. The third option and, in my view, the best one, is to actually differentiate quality of services requirements within the networks and to cater in that sense to the quality requirements of the different services. But that may violate the net neutrality requirements. So you may not get net neutrality, because you are going to offer different qualities of service and some services may be taking a backseat. At the same time quality-of-service differentiation can of course be used by networks to differentiate their service combinations against each other and therefore reduce competition. Obviously, under full net neutrality you are going to homogenize the networks, and therefore the service competition between networks may become fierce.

3.2. Pricing

Now I move from quality of service to pricing, beginning with interconnection services. Before convergence interconnection for the telephone service was largely sold on a per-minute basis. Cable TV did not have network interconnection at all. In contrast, the internet backbones had two types of pricing. The first one was peering, which amounted largely to "bill and keep", meaning that they had an agreement to interconnect and the payment was essentially in kind. One network was providing interconnection for the other and vice versa. The second type consisted of for-fee transit arrangements that were largely capacity based and bit based in their pricing.

Let us now turn to the end users. In the telephone networks and wireless networks they largely pay monthly fees and are subject to per minute pricing for usage; the calling-party-pays principle dominates in the countries of Europe and worldwide in the fixed networks, but in the mobile networks there are some countries like the US that have adhered to the receiving-party-pays principle. Typically there is a high willingness to pay for use. So usage pricing can be applied to differentiate or to discriminate between high and low willingness-to-pay consumers. Cable TV companies charge monthly fees for broadcast baskets and there exist payment-on-demand services. The two-sidedness of markets means that advertisers also pay. There is a high willingness to pay for special content. Data and internet have largely been subjected to bandwidth pricing on a monthly basis, complemented by advertising or capacity based usage pricing. There is a high willingness to pay for access. Essentially the willingness to pay in the internet is for bandwidth.

The convergence is associated with large investments: Some of those required for NGN maybe questionable, but there are large investments out there. The networks have to finance these investments. Here two properties come together: first, the new types of networks are associated with more fixed costs and sunk costs relative to variable costs. Fibre lines require less maintenance than copper lines and are more capital intensive. Similar properties hold for access lines and for the NGN networks. Thus, very large fixed investments need to be financed, but under the convergence model the network operators may lose part of their ability to finance them through usage based pricing. The predominant pricing model moves away from usage-based pricing and that basks the question, where should we get the money from. This is where part of the net neutrality debate is rooted, which is: okay, let's try to get the money from content or from service providers. Per-minute pricing is no longer useful in an all-IP world. We therefore expect a potential move to capacity based pricing and bill and keep in the interconnection part and already see flat-rate pricing in the end-user part. A big countervailing debate in the US has, however, emerged about usage pricing for the internet. The whole discussion about Comcast blocking certain high capacity use came about, because they argued that they don't have enough capacity in place and that the high users should pay. Apparently, a new model of usage based pricing on the internet is in the making. But it essentially started via violation of net neutrality. In reaction to public outcry the carriers are currently trying out new pricing models with voluntary participants.

3.3 Content Providers

What has been the role of content providers before convergence? One can argue that in telephone networks the content providers always have been the users themselves. The net neutrality issue really did not arise here, except if one takes the view that the calling-party-pays principle is essentially a violation of net neutrality, because it makes the caller pay for what are 2-sided benefits. The whole termination monopoly issue, which you may be familiar with, arises because only the caller pays. The network that delivers the call has a monopoly on delivery, because the call can go only to this particular user. In cable TV the content provision was to some extend vertically integrated or provided directly by independent content providers and there were some broadcasting networks with advertising financing. The major net neutrality issue here concerned the must-carry rules.

In the traditional internet the content was partly vertically integrated, but mostly separated from the networks. So we have vertically integrated models, like in Germany with Deutsche Telekom, and content was largely paid by advertisement fee. In the past there was no big net neutrality issue. After convergence, however, the content providers are in quite differentiated positions. You have content provision by outside content providers and by end user (youtube). There is a large increase in content provision by end users and there are also vertically integrated internet service providers (ISPs) that provide their own content and in part have their walled gardens.

The network has to attract complementary users in order to enhance network effects. The networks are interested in getting customers—the customers are interested in content, so the network which can provide content in certain ways will get more users. That has two effects: one is that it limits the exclusion of content so that the networks want to provide a wide variety of content in order to cater to all the users. At the same time they also want to have content exclusively for themselves in order to limit the other networks from providing to all users and this gives some content providers market power vis-à-vis the networks.

4. Convergence, Competition and Net Neutrality

Now let me move on to the relationship between convergence, competition and net neutrality. I will concentrate largely on Figure 1 below. We have so far only dealt with the right side of the graph. That is we have looked at convergence leading to more heterogeneous, multi-product networks. That would naturally result in less net neutrality. I now want to move to the left side, starting with the logic behind it. Convergence also increases network competition, because now the different networks that had monopolies before have been converging. They are now offering the same services so that several networks are now competing with each other. That increases network competition and that reduces the bargaining power of the individual networks against content providers. It also provides less incentive to exclude content providers. These factors together would lead to more net neutrality. Overall, Figure 1 presents a tension between these two tendencies.

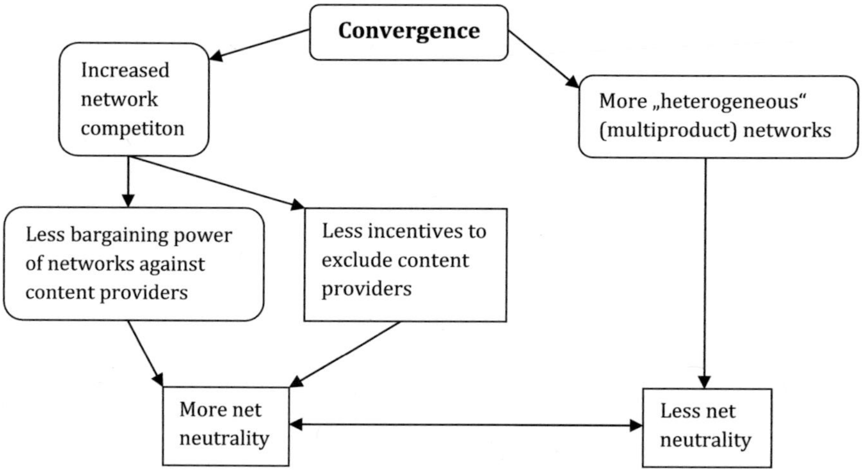

Figure 1: Convergence, Competition and Net Neutrality

The right side leads to less net neutrality; the left side leads to more net neutrality. This view still is incomplete, because obviously the networks do not have an interest in more competition. They want less of it. One way to actually lessen competition is to reduce net neutrality. That is, by reducing net neutrality they can differentiate their network services from each other via content. So via differentiated content the networks are able to lessen competition and therefore they have an incentive to violate net neutrality.

5. Policy Conclusions

Moving on to policy conclusions, I want to argue that there are only two main policy options for net neutrality. Those are competition policy or net neutrality regulation. Competition policy is the fallback, because in network industries at least some market power is typically present. We cannot exclude competition policy. The policy maker cannot say I don't do anything. Net neutrality violations fall squarely in the realm of competition policy, where they may or may not count as violations. They are discriminations of some kind, such as quality discrimination or price discrimination, and in some cases the networks are going to decline service to someone. These discriminations are intrinsically linked to competition policy. So the policy options only include net neutrality regulation and competition policy. The question is under what circumstances, which one is to be preferred.

A criterion for the desirable ability of net neutrality regulations is that the unregulated market—only subject to general competition law—generates a lower level of welfare than under net neutrality regulation. That would be the reason for having regulation; if the welfare is expected to be lower under competition law only then you prefer regulation. There is a question mark about the policy objective being either general social welfare or consumer welfare. Economists in the past have generally preferred the measure of social welfare which includes consumer welfare and the profit of the firm. But there has been a tendency, in particular in competition law, to move to a long term consumer benefits standard. This assumes either that the profits are dissipated in the long run, meaning that firms only receive returns for risk taking but not for market power, or that the laws applying both to competition and regulation typically address the consumers as the weaker parties.

In any type of policy decision one can make two types of errors. One can accept the wrong or one can reject the right. This begs the question: where are we going to make the bigger mistakes? More precisely, if we do not regulate is this going to end in a catastrophe; is that the bigger mistake or is the bigger mistake that if we regulate we may strangle the market. These two types of consequences have to be weighted with probabilities. How likely is it under each policy that we make a big mistake? Those are the properties to be taken in mind. Together with Jürgen Kühling and others, I developed a scheme of looking at regulation and at competition law in view of what differentiates the two. The main properties of regulation are (1) ex ante intervention, (2) a specialised agency and (3) prescriptive intervention. That is the regulator does not just say no, but actually spells out what should be done. This refers to pricing and quality setting and is associated with advantages and drawbacks, each one of them. In particular, advantages of ex ante intervention are its immediacy, precision, dependability and prevention. But it has the drawback of reducing substantially the freedom to compete. You take away the freedom to compete and therefore you pay for the advantages with over-intervention. The regulator as a specialized agency has specialized knowledge. It can intervene more speedily. But the drawback is that there are interest groups that influence the outcome and that can lead to too little or too much intervention, depending on which of the interest groups prevail: the ones who want less or the ones who want more. The prescriptive intervention again is likely ex ante to provide more precision and stronger influence on the desired behaviour. So, that is the good news. The bad news is again that it takes away the freedom to do the right thing and may carry severe mistakes in doing so.

Now consider the corresponding properties of competition law. One is that the competition authority has to show that there is a violation. Competition policy therefore mostly works ex post. The second property of competition law is that the courts and the competition agencies are unable to affirmatively set prices. They can say, this is a discriminating price, but they cannot say what the right price would have to be and if they could they would not able to supervise it in the long run. As a consequence competition law may be inappropriate if there are large and irreparable damages. If one has to show a violation and the damage has been catastrophic already, then that may not be helpful. Sometimes it is difficult to prove abuses. This holds for the case of predation or if frequent and repeated abuses are likely. High frequency of abuses and catastrophic outcomes do not appear to apply to net neutrality. Rather, my judgement is that net neutrality violations tend to be rare and it is unlikely for individual violations of net neutrality to become catastrophic. We have only very few net neutrality cases so far. The inability of competition authorities to set prices is also not very applicable to the net neutrality issue, because price discrimination has yet to become a major net neutrality issue. The inability of supervision would be relevant in case of very high information requirements and continuous supervision requirements. Again, that doesn't seem to be highly relevant for net neutrality, although quality discrimination would need some supervision.

Let me come to the final conclusions. I hope to have convinced you that net neutrality poses a fairly complex issue and that it is quite difficult to evaluate the outcomes. But that precisely makes ex ante policies or per se rules unlikely to be optimal. Achieving net neutrality is hardly so good that we should prescribe it under all circumstances. But there are cases where it may be better to have some differentiation or discrimination. Those circumstances should be brought out in individual cases rather than with some brush that says: okay, we forbid everything. I make one possibly general exception. There should be some transparency requirements for quality of service. Because the quality-of-service differentiation, once it comes, will be very hard for consumers to decide on. In that case a particular danger is that, by providing a superior service, the networks may also want to deteriorate the current service. So the standard service in the internet would be best effort. But they could deteriorate the best effort service, so as to make it more attractive for people to move to the superior service. However, being forced to publish their quality of service may induce the networks to become more competitive on the quality front. That would, hopefully, let only reasonable discrimination survive.

Protection of Confidential Business Data in the Age of Convergence

Indra Spiecker gen. Döhmann

1. Introduction

When talking about protection of data, one usually thinks of one particular field: the especially recently highly accentuated area of data protection, i.e. the protection of person-related private information.[1] Such private information is highly guarded against third-party access and use. Many constitutions even provide for a specific basic individual right to data privacy[2] because personal information is considered to be a core legal right of the individual in many countries. Its value originates not only in the individual's interests, but also in its importance for the functioning of many other basic individual rights. Thus, it is considered to be an important backbone of any democratic and free society: Data protection prevents—among other things—the unauthorized collection and observation of data and thus the exploitation of private information.[3] As good as this seems in theory for the protection of private information, there are as many obstacles to assuring this protection in practice. One of the major problems lies in the effectiveness of legal protection: How can the individual ensure that his/her personal information is not used by someone else without valid authorization or explicit consent?[4] This question has become pressuring due to the technical developments in information society: Digitalization, the Internet, the speed and means of communication, the convergence of content and infrastructure also change the access, the availability, the re-organization, and ultimately also the means of protecting information.

This paper, however, looks at another field of data protection. It is a kind of data protection that has undeservedly spent far less time in the spotlight of the media, economy and law: the protection of confidential[5] business data. It is still not clear under which national, European and/or international constitutional right such business data is protected and to

[1] On the European as well as national levels, e.g. the EC data retention directive of 2006 has been intensively discussed.

[2] See Art. 2 sect. 2, Art. 1 sect. 1 of the German Constitution Grundgesetz (Basic Law (GG)), the so-called right to informational self-determination, or Art. 8 sect. 1 of the European Convention on Human Rights (ECHR)—data protection as part of the right to privacy.

[3] See the German Constitutional Court (Bundesverfassungsgericht) in its ground-breaking decision of 1983, BVerfGE 65, 1 = Neue Juristische Wochenschrift (NJW) 1984, p. 419.

[4] Compare Directive 95/46/EG and its transfer into national laws, e.g. the German Federal and State Data Protection Laws.

[5] The term is not used in a uniform way—other terms applied are "secret business information" and "private business information".

what extent. However, the problems raised here are just as threatening—if not more so—to core interests and core legal rights, namely those of constitutionally protected legal entities. This is true especially for highly innovative industries such as telecommunications, broadcasting, the Internet and media—the industries involved in the convergence processes.

In the long run, the unprotected use of business information can pose a threat to a free, self-determined society similar to that posed by the uncontrolled use of personal data. Without protection of business data, the development of business activities and a market economy cannot take place freely. Market failure is certain, and lack of innovation is typical because anyone who cannot protect the advantages of his or her business and ideas will refrain from investment—and certainly from investment in new information, new technology, or new procedures. The possible economic consequences for society are manifold; the legal interests of many companies can easily be violated by private and state infringements on the protection of business information. Thus, the legal framework for the protection of business data plays an important role in the development and design of technical possibilities. Where new technology produces new business ideas and extends into existing business fields, the protection of the ideas behind it becomes crucial for the businesses involved.

This is true—and can be observed—particularly in the field of digital convergence: From the technical side, convergence offers a highly innovative and creative field. Thus, new information plays an important role and is the potentially decisive factor in the market position of the involved players and industries. Therefore, business data protection is of vital interest for the further development of this market. From the legal standpoint, digital convergence links several legal fields, classically telecommunications, the Internet (media), and broadcasting. Data protection is part of the overlaying legal structure that governs all of these legal fields. It has to be designed and interpreted in order to enable the technical innovations to be possible, feasible, and usable and still protect the involved business data. Therefore, data protection of business information and innovation go hand in hand.[6]

The protection of personal data and the protection of business data share a similar starting point: Private persons and business persons alike have a strong interest in keeping information about themselves to themselves. Both want to control who knows what about

[6] See on this aspect e.g. Martin Eifert/Wolfgang Hoffmann-Riem (Eds.), Innovationsfördernde Regulierung, Berlin 2009.

them. However, the ways in which the two kinds of data are protected differ significantly.[7] Therefore, the question should be raised whether the standard of protection in personal data is similar to the standard of protection in business data provided for by national, European, and international law—and we should also ask what the institutions how to protect business data can learn from the institutions how to protect private data. These and the related questions of a unified data protection standard can, however, only be answered by looking into the many different aspects involved, not least the effects on innovation. This paper does not aim at developing a general system of data protection. Rather, it concentrates on analyzing the present legal framework under which convergence-related business data is protected and examines which unsolved problems threaten innovative processes from the data protection angle. Therefore, it looks at the general material and procedural standards by which business data as such is protected and illustrates some of the effects of this regulation. One particular problem—i.e. the conflict between disclosure laws and competitors' rights on the one hand and the protection of confidential business information on the other hand—will be scrutinized.

With respect to the field of telecommunications, the German Constitutional Court ruled in 2006 that the standard for protection of confidential business information granted by administrative law was not yet sufficient and therefore required a higher standard.[8] However, it did not elaborate on the exact outline of this higher standard. Also, its argumentation excluded one particular recent development in the law: Freedom of Information Laws now grant free access to government information. This right of one person and any potential protection of private business data of another person may collide. This is especially true in regulated industries such as telecommunications and broadcasting, because in this case an administrative agency becomes an important holder of business information in the course of enacting regulation standards, and this agency is required to disclose its information according to the Freedom of Information laws. The general scheme is similar in most European countries, as telecommunication has been the target of the European Community's harmonization, liberalization, and privatization efforts. And the legal issues at stake are very similarly defined: Property, business, freedom of information, and

[7] The difference in the perception of these rights is even greater: While most companies are very much aware of the importance of the protection of their business data, many individuals are quite generous in distributing their personal information.

[8] German Constitutional Court Decision, BVerfGE 115, 205 ff. = Deutsches Verwaltungsblatt (DVBl) 2006, p. 694 = Neue Zeitschrift für Verwaltungsrecht (NVwZ) 2006, p. 1041 = Multimedia und Recht (MMR) 2006, p. 375.

anti-corruption-measures make up the core interests weighted against each other. Therefore, although this paper will refer to the German national legal situation, the analysis and its conclusions can easily be transferred to the legal situation of other European countries, even to the U.S.

The first part (2.) will give a general outline of the present legal protection of confidential business data (2.1.). This part will further describe the different relationships of the parties potentially involved and the legal parameters under which they operate (2.2.). It will finally examine the conflict of protection of confidential business information with the Freedom of Information Laws (2.3.) and then go on to outline a solution according to the individual value of the information (2.4.). The final Outlook section will stress the need for an international solution (3.).

2. Protection of Confidential Business Data

2.1. Definition of Confidential Business Data

Confidential Business Data is defined in public and private law in the same way: It consists of any and all relevant pieces of business-related information that are not publicly accessible and that are available only to a restricted number of people according to the will of the business owner.[9] Thus, the critical factor is the business owner's will. He or she decides whether or not a given piece of information is business data that needs protection under the law. Therefore, information freely accessible on the Internet, e.g. on a company's homepage, is not something that is protected as confidential information—because the owner of the information has chosen to make it publicly available.[10]

Protection of business data is of particular interest if a company's advantage over its competitors and its market strength rely on technical developments rather than on service or experience. In this case, the competitive advantage derives from the company's superior information relative to its market competitors. Loss of this relevant business data is therefore the equivalent of a significant loss of competitiveness and ultimately even of business itself.

[9] See only the German Constitutional Court, BVerfG, in: Deutsches Verwaltungsblatt (DVBl) 2006, p. 694, 695 = Neue Zeitschrift für Verwaltungsrecht (NVwZ) 2006, p. 1041, 1042 = Multimedia und Recht (MMR) 2006, p. 375, 376.

[10] It might still need protection with respect to authenticity. This is not topic of this paper.

The field of confidential business information is vast. Confidential business information thus covers any innovation within a business, for example a new technology, a new procedure, or a new chemical. But the term also extends to other information as well, e.g. organizational and financial structures within a company, a new concept for marketing or product distribution, and any future strategy. It also includes information intertwined with personal information, e.g. the salary structure of the employees or the professional networks, the lists of competitors, or the history of contracts with customers and their fulfilment. With regard to convergence, confidential business information covers for example a company's economic evaluation of the industries involved, the technical predispositions, information about the network of individual business prospects in the convergence markets, or the assessment of the competitors' interests. The decision of a company to refrain from joining a network or to invest in the development of convergence structures would be further examples. Most of this information can be of great value to a potential competitor, to the regulator, and to other interested parties.

2.2. Standard of Protection of Confidential Business Data

2.2.1. Private Law

In private law, business data is not absolutely protected, but only in certain aspects and—almost more importantly—only for a limited duration. Intellectual property protection through patent, copyright, or trademark law provides a general shield under which business information can prosper. This is because these laws are unified by the common understanding that the protection of information fosters innovation: It creates property rights, and the existence of these rights prevents the negative effects of the common good that information would otherwise be.[11] Without protection of information, everybody could freely use it once it has become available—and the institution having invested in creating this information would not be able to receive adequate compensation. In the long run, information would not be produced. However, it is also generally known that too much protection hinders innovation by preventing new information from being dispersed. Protection of business information in private law therefore always leads to a balancing of both interests.[12]

[11] On the general theory of common goods, see Richard Cornes/Todd Sandler, The Theory of Externalities, Public Goods and Club Goods, 2nd ed., 1996.

[12] See Rolf Stürner, Juristenzeitung (JZ) 1985, p. 453 ff.

2.2.2. Public Law

In public law, the protection of confidential business data has not yet been conclusively defined. Governments need knowledge in order to act; knowledge of past, present and future provides legitimacy of state decisions. Therefore, the government typically requires private actors to disclose information from their sphere to the government in order to dissolve any information asymmetry on the side of the government. However, the general question of whether and to what extent constitutional safeguards exist against the state's interest in business data and how they determine administrative law remains unresolved. Special administrative laws present highly specified criteria that stipulate under which conditions the information has to be shared. These laws usually do not specify compensation for the loss of the confidential information: The addressee of a regulation simply has to accept the loss of (some of) his or her business secrets to the state. The reason for this lies in the state's interest in the information: The main goal of the existing regulation is usually not to balance the different interests of two private parties, unlike in private law. Rather, there exists an overruling public interest in the information in order to address a further public interest: The administrative agency is e.g. interested in the cost to the incumbent for providing network services. This is not because of the information itself, but because the agency wants to overcome market failure structures in a particular market segment of telecommunications.

There is another reason why compensation for the provision of confidential information is often not considered necessary in the state-private party relationship. It is founded on the idea of the state as an unconditional keeper of the secret information. The state is not allowed to pass on the information; therefore, the private party is still considered completely protected. The law creates the illusion that the information is as safe as with the state as with the private party itself.[13]

Thus, the general level of protection of confidential business information differs considerably in public and private law, depending on the context and the actors involved: If it is a private person requiring access to company information, private laws may grant access in order to foster general innovation. At the same time, they also grant the innovator certain rights, e.g. privileges or fees in order to grant him or her at least some of the economic advantages of the innovation. In general, the disclosure of knowledge against the will of the

[13] That this is just an illusion has been shown by reality many times. Bad intent is not necessarily the source of data loss; one should recall the accidental loss of a CD by a British government official holding the social security data of thousands of British citizens.

innovator, i.e. the keeper of the business information, is the exception. However, if it is the state that requires access to company information, public laws may grant access to it in order to further the public interest. Compensation is not granted—and innovation is just one of the many public interests involved. In general, the disclosure of knowledge to the government against the will of the innovator, i.e. the keeper of the business information, is the rule.

2.3. The Effects of the Freedom of Information Laws on the Protection of Confidential Business Information

2.3.1. Freedom of Information Laws

This general understanding in public law has been changed by the Freedom of Information Laws. This is particularly true with respect to the concept of the state as a safe keeper of secrets; the state no longer acts as a safe harbour for information in this case but rather as a distributor to the general public. This is because the Freedom of Information Laws enable third, generally disinterested parties to request any information stored by the state. These laws do not require the claimant to show any legally acknowledged interest. The legislative intent behind these laws is to uphold the general public interest: By making a request, the claimant serves the public interest in transparency of state decisions and their controllability. The existence of these laws consequently changes the way that protection of business information has to be considered, as information available to the state mostly consists of information about business and personal interests rather than of information about the state itself. Thus, the Freedom of Information Laws give access not only to state information, but also to private and business information.

2.3.2. The Protection of Confidential Business Information within the Freedom of Information Laws

a) Freedom of Information Laws

The Freedom of Information Laws regularly do not leave confidential business information completely unprotected. Rather, they require the administrative agency to which the claim is made to decide on the protection-worthiness of the information in each individual case. In order to do so, the agency has to consult with the owner of the confidential business information to determine whether he or she claims confidentiality.[14] If so, the agency is required to reject the third party's claim completely; the business information stays within the state's arena and its protective shield remains intact. Therefore, the protection of confidential business information does not seem to have been changed[15] i.e. compromised by the Freedom of Information Laws.

b) Environmental Freedom of Information Laws

This is at least the case if the general Freedom of Information Laws are applied. A problem, however, arises from European Law: Under the Environmental Freedom of Information Laws,[16] the protection of business information is not absolute, i.e. does not entail a yes/no decision from the administrative agency. Rather, it requires an evaluation of the interests involved.[17] Therefore, if business information is requested by a third party, the regulatory agency may not directly reject the claim as it would be required to do under the general Freedom of Information Laws. Instead, it is obliged to evaluate whether an additional special public interest resides in the disclosure of the information that might overrule the private interest in maintaining the secrecy of the information. This evaluation may thus lead to the violation of business confidentiality by the state: Although the state and business owner acknowledge the confidentiality of the information, due to overriding motives, the agency nevertheless reveals the information to the third party.

c) Additional Rights to State Information

However, the Freedom of Information Laws are not the only grounds upon which a party may rest its claim to state information. Such further individual rights to disclosure include the right to a fair administrative procedure, to the protection of business interests, and to the protection of competition and property, to name only the most prominent.[18] Most of

---

[14] The business owner is often asked to mark confidential information accordingly when transferring it to the agency so that the consultation process can be avoided. This also solves the problem of the agency having to identify the business information in the first place.

[15] This paper does not consider the effects of the agencies' different self-understandings when interpreting the Freedom of Information Laws: It is quite possible that a more "service-oriented" self-understanding of the agencies might lead to a more lenient approach to protection.

[16] In Germany, this is called the Umweltinformationsgesetz (UIG). It is based on directives 90/313/EWG and especially on 2003/4/EG and also transfers the Aarhus Convention (Unece Convention on Access to Information, Public Participation in Decision-making and Access to Justice in Environmental Matters), signed 1998, into national law.

[17] Although the Environmental Freedom of Information Act applies only to environmental issues, the European and national courts have interpreted "environmental issue" in a broad sense. Therefore, many issues in the area of convergence are governed by the UIG/European Law.

[18] All of these individual rights are acknowledged by the European Convention on Human Rights and are part of the European Constitution/Treaty of Lisboa; they therefore apply to all European states.

these rights, however, require the direct involvement of the claimant in the government decision in which the information was used. This is decidedly *not* the case in Freedom of Information contexts: Here, the claimant need not have any particular involvement. He need not be part of the administrative procedure.

d) The Use of Freedom of Information Laws by Competitors

The clear-cut general rule—protection and some compensation if information is shared among private parties under a private law regime; protection and generally no compensation if information is shared under a public law regime with the state—[19] becomes questionable in most of the situations convergence touches upon. The Freedom of Information Laws can become the gateway for competitors to use administrative agencies to gather information.

d1) The Problem

The situation arises in all competition-regulating decision-making—and therefore often in the areas convergence touches upon: telecommunications, media, broadcasting, and Internet regulation. Here, regulatory decisions concerning one party often necessarily influence another party's competitive position, predominantly because this other party is a competitor. The outcome of a regulatory decision in regulated markets changes the competitive environment not only for the direct party of the regulatory decision (e.g. the incumbent), but also for all other competitors. For example, in telecommunications, the regulatory agency has to rule on the price for certain telecommunication services set by an incumbent in order to control market conditions, e.g. the price that has to be paid by any competitor using an existing network. Therefore, the other party is highly interested in all of the information upon which the regulatory agency based its decision. This information consists of general knowledge (about the market itself, general technical developments, and general regulatory guidelines in the field of convergence) as well as highly specific knowledge regarding the particular decision (about the strategy, the price politics, investments, technical innovations, and company standards). This particular information is mostly directly linked to the addressee of the regulatory decision. Therefore, knowledge obtained by the competitor about the agency's specific knowledge in the particular case often means knowledge about the addressee of the decision—and thus about a major

[19] See supra 2.2. 1. and 2.

competitor. Knowing the strategy, the portfolio, and the investments of a competitor can turn a failing business into the market leader.[20]

This seems to imply that seeking information about a competitor is at least doubtful, potentially morally questionable, and maybe even illegal. But a company can rightfully claim a legally accepted and protected interest in the information.[21] As the information is the basis of the regulatory agency's decision, a business can only effectively control this decision if it has access to the information. Therefore, the right to know this information is indubitable—as is the incumbent's or addressee's right not to share information.

d2) Legal Setting

Legislation is not unaware of this problem. It tries to diminish it with certain provisions that grant the competitor the right to control the regulatory agency, but also allows for the protection of the other party's confidential business information. The way to achieve this is usually to transfer the problem to the procedural (and court) level rather than to directly provide guidelines for a decision on the material level.

For example, the German Telecommunications Act (TKG) provides for the distribution of information only if it has previously been blackened. This means that the addressee can decide what the competitor may know; his rights are thus fully protected. Therefore, the addressee of the regulatory decision has a strong interest in blackening as much as possible. The competitor's interest, however, aims at having as little as possible blackened, as every blackened piece of information hinders his or her evaluation of the decision—and consequently, the chances of success in challenging the regulatory decision are considerably diminished. The competitor is unable to decide from this standpoint whether the regulatory decision is questionable and on what grounds. But the problem doesn't end there: The competitor is also unable to present his case in court, as he or she can usually challenge only the legal aspects without referring to the factual grounds.

Therefore, the German Administrative Court Procedure Act provides for a so-called "in-camera-proceeding".[22] It creates an intermediate proceeding in court: A chamber of the court that is not the deciding chamber independently evaluates whether or not the confidential business information is truly confidential and thus whether the administrative

[20] Therefore, industrial espionage not only targets product information, but also—and to a greater extent—development information.

[21] This is when the other rights to state information come into play; see also supra 2.3.2. c).

[22] § 99 sect. 2 Administrative Court Procedure Act (Verwaltungsgerichtsordnung (VwGO)).

agency's decision to withhold the information was lawful. The result of this finding is then entered accordingly in the main process: If the intermediate court finds the information protection-worthy, the competitor has to argue his or her case without it; if the court does not find the information to be protection-worthy, then the competitor is granted free access to it and can change his or her claim accordingly. Thus, the interests of both parties are acknowledged and balanced.

d3) Further Unresolved Questions

This solution sounds like a reasonable, maybe even elegant, way to protect confidential business information and at the same time serve as an effective means of controlling regulatory agency decision-making by all affected parties.[23]

Procedural solutions, like blackening critical information and letting an independent court control the confidentiality decision of the administrative agency, however, do not yet fully take into account the constitutional dimensions involved. And within the field of convergence, there may well be even more constitutional positions to be considered.

So far, the problem has mostly been viewed as concerning the addressee's (incumbent's) rights, deriving from the protection of his or her business confidentiality. It is generally agreed that these rights are protected under the Constitution, although it is not clear under which provisions.[24] On the competitor's side, the constitutionality of his or her position has not been clearly identified aside from possible protection under the right of protection of profession and competition,[25] as the regulatory agency's decision infringes on his or her right to free participation in the market. However, the very moment he or she enters into a court proceeding to control the regulatory agency´s decision, his or her constitutional right to a legal hearing[26] and effective protection against state decisions[27] strengthen his or her constitutional position. This has so far not been properly acknowledged.[28]

[23] According to the German Constitutional Court, BVerfGE 115, 205 ff., upholding § 99 sect. 2 VwGO.

[24] Art. 12 sect. 1 (protection of profession and competition) and Art. 14 sect. 1 (protection of property) of the German Constitution (GG), are probable rights; the Constitutional Court has left open which of them was violated.

[25] Under German Constitutional Law, this would be Art. 12 sect. 1 GG.

[26] Under German Constitutional Law, this would be Art. 20 sect. 3 GG.

[27] Under German Constitutional Law, this would be Art. 19 sect. 4 GG.

[28] This does not necessarily imply a different solution; it may turn out that the protection of the confidentiality of the business interests still requires a solution similar to the one provided today. However, the decision-making process of the legislature—and the critique of the German Constitutional Court—does not yet take these rights into account.

The situation becomes even more difficult, however, if one takes the Freedom of Information rights into account. In constitutions that provide for freedom to publicly accessible information like the German Constitution,[29] these laws do not merely grant the individual a general right to information from the government; they have also actually changed the constitution insofar as they declare all state information to be publicly accessible information.[30] Therefore, the position of the competitor is significantly strengthened, because he or she can now not only claim a violation of business protection rights and of the rights to a legal hearing and effective protection, but now additionally a violation of the constitutionally granted right to information if the confidentiality of the incumbent's information is protected. This also calls for a re-balancing the interests involved.

2.4. A Solution to Protect Confidential Business Information

This situation calls for a different solution for balancing the individual interests involved in each case rather than opting for a general either-or solution. A more differentiated approach is called for. Such a differentiation could arise from the distinct value information can have. Not all business information necessarily shares the same value and importance for a business. This discrepancy could be an important guideline for determining the level of protection. Therefore, only important business information of considerable value for the development of a business should be strictly protected (and then even more so than it is today). In these cases, the rights of the business owner prevail; he or she is granted strict protection. Other, less valuable information—which is not to say that knowledge of this information would not influence competition—could then be treated differently. Here, the rights of the competitor (or the general public) may prevail.

The threshold then becomes a factual rather than a legal threshold—the significance of information on individual business prospects. In this context, only a general outline can be given regarding what would constitute cues for separating business information into the "important" and "less important" categories.[31] One cue is the business's degree of investment in developing the new information: High levels of investment would call for a

---

[29] Under German Constitutional Law, this would be Art. 5 sect. 1 GG ("Informationsfreiheit").

[30] Most commentaries on the German Freedom of Information Law (Informationsfreiheitsgesetz (IFG)) agree on this.

[31] The line can be drawn according to the different standards of protection under Art. 12 sect. 1 and Art. 14 sect. 1 GG. Business information that is protected under the high standard of Art. 12 sect. 1 will therefore need a higher level of protection in all legal areas other than business information under the regular standard of Art. 12 sect. 1 and 14 sect. 1 GG. In this context, a differentiated legal construction will be neglected. It can be found in Indra Spiecker gen. Doehmann, Der Schutz von Betriebs- und Geschäftsgeheimnissen (protection of confidential business information), forthcoming.

higher degree of protection. Another cue is the concreteness of the possibilities that the information opens up: Possibilities that are not yet definable and still call for further, fairly broad and open research usually deserve less protection than possibilities that are on the verge of being transformed into concrete business plans. One useful cue evaluates the re-combination of the information: A high degree of potential would call for greater protection. Another cue builds upon the business strategy itself: If the information is vital for business development, it enjoys a higher degree of protection. Therefore, a business with a small portfolio may in the end receive more protection than a multi-level business. Several other cues can be identified. Finally, a single piece of information may need less protection than a whole bundle of information.

These, of course, provide only general guidelines and general cues that allow for a more differentiated evaluation. This evaluation has to take into account that some of these characteristics may be present at the same time. For example, a single piece of information that is central for an entire strategy might very well enjoy the highest protection standards. However, these cues allow for a certain standardization of a balancing of interests that may then include other, secondary interests as well—such as the furthering of innovation within society as such. In the end, they provide predictability for all parties involved and a differentiated solution to legislation as well: Legal standards may embrace both material and procedural protection.

3. Outlook

Protection of highly innovative business information such as in the field of convergence is becoming increasingly difficult. At the same time, it is becoming increasingly necessary for the businesses to develop their future portfolios and future successes in a fast-changing media environment. The issues raised here will thus become important in the regulation of convergence markets. Constitutional positions call for a more standardized and at the same time more differentiated decision between the protection of confidential information and protection of rightful competitors' and the public's interests. Such a solution may rest in the different value the required piece of information has.

One of the major advantages lies in the possibility of the globalized protection that convergence requires: As information can be transferred within seconds, and local connections become less important, a differentiation that carries across borders into the international setting is necessary. Therefore, the protection of confidential business interests is not only a national or European issue, but rather a global issue for the business world today. The industries involved in digital convergence are aware of the quick transferability of information, the fast development of technology and the importance of innovation. It is their core business to protect their innovative standard. This has to be guaranteed—through awareness of the insufficient and thus far different national, European, and international levels of legal protection.

Part 2: Convergence & Digital Dividend

Auctioning the Digital Dividend

Peter Cramton

1. Introduction

Today I am going to talk about auctioning the digital dividend. More broadly I am going to talk about auctions, and even more broadly I am going to talk about market design. The basic idea of market design is to establish the rules of market interaction for the market participants consistent with the objectives of the market maker. It can be viewed as economic engineering, and typically relies on many disciplines. In fact my initial training was as an engineer, but the primary fields that are used are economics, computer science, and operations research. Market design can be broken down into two categories: matching problems where we don´t use prices, such as matching medical interns to hospitals, students to schools, or kidneys to patients, and auctions were we do use prices.

I would argue that market design fosters innovation by improving price formation, enhancing competition, and mitigating market failure. In my mind a good mantra for regulators is "make markets work better." Thus, the commissioners at the FCC in the United States should strive to determine how they can design the regulation to make the markets work better, identifying where there are market failures and stepping in to address them as directly and simply as possible. This process of finding or anticipating market failures and addressing them with effective market rules is what market design is all about.

There are many examples of market design applications utilizing auctions. Recently I have worked on auctions for emission allowances, airport slots, radio spectrum, electricity, gas, timber, and rough diamonds.

Today I am going to focus on spectrum auctions, but another application that I spent a lot of time on this fall is the global financial crisis. US Treasury Secretary Henry Paulson initially had a Plan A that involved auctioning the mortgage-related securities or toxic assets of the banks. The Treasury intended to buy some $700 billion of the toxic assets, and a law passed in the United States to do just that. I became involved in the development of Plan A at the end of September, but then at the end of October the Treasury decided not to auction, but instead to bailout the banks on a bank-by-bank basis. Now we appear to be going to Plan C were the Treasury may return to using an auction. So eventually it will happen, but my view is that auctions would have been a very good thing in the context of the financial crisis. The crisis was caused by mispricing: investment bankers were able to sell poor securities for full value based on misleading ratings. This mispricing was supported by the absence of a transparent secondary market for these mortgage-related securities. If we had transparent prices, a lot of the bad things that happened would not have happened. In particular the housing bubble would have been much less, and the investment bankers would not have been able to make such clever use of the rating agencies and create tens-of-thousands of senseless securities obfuscating prices. Even a tiny bit of good market design would have averted the financial crisis by preventing its root cause: the sale of subprime mortgages as near-riskless securities.

But I am not here to talk about the financial crisis and its resolution. I am here to talk about spectrum auctions, and in particular how spectrum auctions can be employed with respect to the digital dividend. As a result of digital technology, we have lots of TV broadcast spectrum that can be freed up for better use. This is the digital dividend. Auctions are the best approach to ensuring that the spectrum is put to its best use. However, auctions are not the only instrument. Some spectrum should be set aside for common property use. For spectrum applications that do not create additional scarcity, the commons model is better than the auction model. There are many examples of this: garage door openers, car locks, and other device controllers. This use requires little bandwidth or power, and thus, does not make the spectrum scarce. Scarcity problems are mitigated by operator separation. In contrast, mobile phones require much greater power and bandwidth, creating spectrum scarcity, and hence an auction is needed to allocate the scarce resource.

In the US, we have about 435 MHz of spectrum devoted to TV broadcast. This is prime, beach-front, spectrum with outstanding propagation properties for all sorts of communications. Broadcasters are scheduled to switch to digital-only transmission in February 2009 (postponed to June), freeing up large blocks of the spectrum for other use. Europe is planning a similar digital dividend. In fact, countries have been slow to release spectrum for mobile communications and other high-value uses creating a false scarcity of spectrum, and higher auction prices than would have occurred if countries pursued more aggressive plans to free up new spectrum. Nonetheless, the auctioning of spectrum has made countries aware of how important it is to manage the spectrum resource well. This is seen in both the developed and developing economies of the world. Effective communications policy is a cornerstone of economic development.

The spectrum auction application is an exciting one, and it has been going on for some time. The first spectrum auctions took place beginning in July of 1994 in the United States. It is an interesting problem, because in a spectrum auction one is auctioning many things that are heterogeneous but similar. There are competing technologies that could be used by operators to provide a wide range of communication services. As a result, the setting has a complex structure of substitutes and complements. This is a long-term investment market, because the operators that are buying the spectrum are building networks, and building a network is an extremely expensive operation—one that the operator is going to do on a long-term basis.

The goal for the government should be efficiency, not revenue maximization. The government should focus on ensuring that those who can put the spectrum to its highest use get it. Focusing simply on revenue maximization is short-sighted. Some measures such as technical and service flexibility and aggregation of licenses can enable more efficient use which could increase auction revenues. But short-run revenue maximization by creating monopolies, which would create the highest profits before spectrum fees, and therefore would sustain the largest fees should be resisted. Indeed, competition, which ultimately will lead to greater innovation and better and cheaper services, will likely generate *greater* government revenues from a long-run perspective. The government can best accomplish this objective with an efficient auction, putting the spectrum to its best use.

There are large inefficiencies—and I do not mean technical inefficiencies, I mean economic inefficiencies—where spectrum is not being put to its best use. We need to do better. The digital dividend is a wonderful example of where we have a large amount of the highest quality spectrum for communication purposes. This spectrum is now devoted to an increasingly low-value use—broadcast television. Broadcast TV is increasingly low-value because the vast majority of people are not getting their TV from over-the-air broadcast, rather most receive their TV signals from cable or satellite. There is a tremendous opportunity to make better use of this TV spectrum, an opportunity that has been a long time coming.

The regulator may find it necessary to introduce spectrum caps or other preferences favoring new entrants so as to level the playing field between incumbents and new entrants. Incumbents include in their private value, the benefit of foreclosing competition, thus driving a wedge between social value and private value. In theory the regulator can correct this externality by favoring the new entrant, but in practice this has proven to be difficult. The

FCC's experience with preferences for certain bidders—set asides, bidding credits, and installment payments—has been largely a failure at least with respect to mobile broadband communication, which is where most of the value lies.

In contrast, a good example of successful intervention was Canada's use of a set aside in its 2008 Advanced Wireless Services or AWS auction. As a result, multiple deep-pocketed new entrants came to the auction, and bid up the price of not only the set-aside block, but the non-set-aside blocks. The result was a much more competitive auction (with much higher revenues) and the introduction of some potentially strong new service providers going forward. The approach effectively broke up regional market-splitting by the dominant incumbents. Another successful intervention was the FCC's use of a spectrum cap in early broadband PCS auctions. The cap limited the quantity of spectrum any one operator could hold in a geographic area, addressing the potential market failure of limited competition in the market for wireless services.

Despite these successes in Canada and the US, I believe the FCC's long and troubled history with bidder preferences is an important case study to other countries considering preferences for various parties. Installment payments proved especially problematic, as it led to speculative bidding, bankruptcy, and lengthy delay in the use of the spectrum.

In addition, the regulator must resist the temptation to force more "winners" than the market can efficiently support. Sometimes regulators fragment the spectrum and prohibit aggregation in the auction in an effort to create as many winners as possible. The upcoming 3G spectrum auction in India may be one example. Aggregation up to a suitable competitive constraint is preferred.

2. Three Main Points

There are three main points I wish to emphasize today.

Enhance substitution. First in terms of the auction design, it is important to enhance the substitution across the items that are being sold. Enhanced substitution is accomplished through both the product design—what you are auctioning—and of the auction format. Often in the settings that I deal with, the product design can be just as important as the auction design.

Encourage price discovery. Second, encouraging price discovery is extremely important. We need a dynamic process here, because unlike some situations, in the case of spectrum auctions, there is a lot of uncertainty about what things are worth. The bidders need to do a lot of homework to develop a crude valuation model, and they need the benefit of some collective market insights, which can be revealed in a dynamic auction process, in order to improve their decision-making. The nice thing about a dynamic auction is that through this price process the bidders gradually have their sights focused on the most relevant part of the price space. Focusing bidder decisions on what is relevant is in my mind the biggest source of benefit from the dynamic process. This benefit is generally ignored by economists, because economists assume that the bidders fully understand their valuation models, when in practice bidders almost never have a completely specified valuation model. Yes, they do a lot of homework, but there is still a lot of uncertainty about what exactly things are worth, and how they should be valuing the spectrum. The experience of the 3G spectrum auctions in Europe is a good example. The bids were based more on stock prices in a bubble situation, rather than on solid homework about values.

Induce truthful bidding. The third feature I wish to emphasize is the importance of inducing truthful bidding. This is accomplished in the auction design through an effective pricing rule and an activity rule. The two rules work together to encourage bidders to truthfully express preferences throughout the entire auction. This truthful expression of preferences is what leads to excellent price discovery and ultimately an efficient auction outcome.

A variety of different pricing rules are used in practice. The two most common are pay-as-bid pricing, where you pay what you bid if you are the winner, and for a homogenous product, uniform pricing, where you pay the market clearing price. In the particular applications I am discussing today, we generally do not have clearing prices, because of strong complementarities and heterogeneous items. As a result, we need a new kind of pricing rule. The pricing rule that I will describe in detail later is a generalization of Vickrey´s second-price rule.

I now give a brief overview of the package clock auction I recommend. The approach may appear complex. Some amount of complexity is required given the complex economic problem at hand. Simpler versions, such as a simultaneous clock auction are possible in settings where all bidders intend to use the same technology. This may well be the case in developing countries that are conducting spectrum auctions for a particular use after the technology battles have been resolved from the experience in developed countries.

3. An Overview of the Package Clock Auction

The package clock auction is especially useful in situations where the regulator does not know which technology will make best use of the spectrum. In such cases, the auction itself can determine the ultimate band plan specifying how the spectrum is organized. Such an auction is said to be technology neutral, since it allows the competing technologies to determine the winning technologies, as well as operators. A good example is an auction that accommodates both paired and unpaired technologies, such as LTE and WiMAX, respectively. A package auction is essential in this case, since the two uses require that the spectrum be organized in fundamentally different ways. The package clock auction is an especially simple, yet powerful, auction that lets competitive bids determine the ultimate band plan.

The package clock auction has features to address each of my three main points.

First, the product design simplifies the products whenever possible. For example, if bidders primarily care about the quantity of spectrum won in a geographic area, we auction generic spectrum and the bidders bid for a quantity of spectrum in each area. This simplifies the auction, enhances substitution, and improves competition. The specific assignment of lots is determined in the last stage of the auction, once the critical decisions have been made (who won how much in each area). This approach also allows a technology neutral auction, which lets the spectrum be organized in different ways for the different technologies. Each bidder indicates the quantity of spectrum and the type of use in its bids. In this case, the first stage of the auction determines not only who won how much in each area, but the overall quantity of spectrum allocated for a particular use in the area.

Second, to encourage price discovery, the auction begins with a clock stage. Prices ascend for each product with excess demand until there is no excess demand for any product. This simple and familiar price discovery process works extremely well when bidders have incentives for truthful bidding. In the important case of substitutes, the clock stage determines an efficient assignment together with supporting competitive equilibrium prices. Moreover, complements are handled with no increase in the complexity of the clock process. Each bid in the clock stage is a package bid, so bidders can bid without fear of winning only some of what they need.

The bidders may find that they are unable to express preferences for all desirable packages in the clock stage, so following the clock stage is a supplementary round. Bidders can increase their bids on packages bid in the clock stage and submit new bids on other packages. All the clock stage bids and the supplementary round bids then are run through an optimizer to determine the value maximizing assignment of the spectrum. This is the generic assignment.

Third, to induce truthful bidding, the auction uses closest-to-Vickrey core pricing. The efficient assignment is priced to minimize the bidders' total payments subject to competitive constraints (no group of bidders has offered the seller more). In practice, this often implies Vickrey pricing, ensuring truthful bidding. However, because of complements, there may be one or more competitive constraints that causes the payments to be greater than Vickrey payments for some bidders. In this event, the smallest deviations from Vickrey prices are used. This maximizes incentives for truthful bidding subject to competitive constraints.

To induce truthful bidding throughout the clock stage, an activity rule based on revealed preference is used. This rule encourages bidders to bid in a manner consistent with profit maximization. Deviations from bidding on the most profitable package throughout the clock stage may impose a constraint on subsequent bids, either later in the clock stage or in the supplementary round. To simplify the auction, a simplified revealed preference rule is desirable that maintains the same one-dimensional structure of the traditional activity rule. In particular, every bid in the clock stage or the supplementary stage is constrained by at most a single constraint. This simplified rule encourages straightforward bidding—always bidding on the most profitable package—without complicating the auction.

Once the generic assignments are determined and priced, the specific assignment stage is run. Each winner submits top-up bids for each specific assignment that is better than the winner's worst specific assignment. The bids indicate the incremental value for each feasible alternative. Then an optimization program is run to determine the efficient specific assignment. Again the prices for the specific assignments are closest-to-Vickrey core prices. This concludes the auction.

I begin by describing some of the problems of the simultaneous ascending auction. Then I present the package clock auction, which retains the benefits, while addressing the weaknesses, of the simultaneous ascending auction. I emphasize two essential elements of the package clock auction: the pricing rule and the activity rule. Along the way, I summarize both experimental and field results with the package clock auction.

4. Simultaneous Ascending Auction

The workhorse for spectrum auctions since 1994 has been the simultaneous ascending auction, a simple generalization of the English auction to multiple items in which all items are auctioned simultaneously. Thus, unlike Sotheby's or Christie's auctions in which the items are auctioned in sequence, here all the items are auctioning simultaneously.

The process is as follows. Each item or lot has a price associated with it. Over a sequence of rounds, we ask bidders to raise the bid on any of the lots they find attractive, and we identify the standing high bidder for each lot at the end of every round. We continue this process until nobody is willing to bid any higher. This process was originally proposed by Preston McAfee, Paul Milgrom, and Robert Wilson for the FCC spectrum auctions. Since its introduction in July 1994, the design has undergone numerous enhancements, but the basic design has remained intact in its application worldwide for the vast majority of spectrum auctions.

An important element of the basic design is an activity rule to address the problem of bid sniping—waiting until the last minute to bid seriously. The rule adopted by the FCC and used in all simultaneous ascending auctions to date is a quantity-based rule. In short, the rule states, "if you want to be a big bidder at the end of the auction, you must be a big bidder throughout the auction." You must maintain a level of eligibility, based on the quantity of spectrum you are bidding for, in order to continue with that level of eligibility later on. Thus, you cannot play a snake-in-the-grass strategy where you hold back and wait, and then pounce late in the auction and win without making your true intent known until the last instant.

As mentioned, the simultaneous ascending auction has been with us for a long time. The FCC has conducted 72 simultaneous ascending auctions, since it was introduced in July of 1994. The FCC has gotten very good at conducting the auctions, and the design has worked reasonably well. Nonetheless, it is perhaps surprising how quickly inertia set in. The FCC was initially highly innovative in its choice of design the first time out of the block, but since then they have just made minor incremental improvements in response to obvious and sometimes severe problems with the original simultaneous ascending auction design.

Why has the design held up so well? It is an effective and simple price discovery process. It allows arbitrage across substitutes. It lets bidders piece together desirable packages of items. And, because of the dynamic process, it reduces the winner's curse by revealing common value information during the auction.

But the design does, and has been observed to have, many weaknesses.

- As a result of the pricing rule, there is a strong incentive for large bidders to engage in demand reduction—reducing the quantity demanded before the bidder's marginal value is reached in order to win at lower prices.
- Especially if there is weak competition, bidders have an incentive to engage in tacit collusion. The bidders employ various signaling strategies where they attempt to work out deals through the language of the bids. The goal of the strategies is to divvy-up the items among the bidders at low prices.
- As a result of the activity rule, there are parking strategies. A bidder maintains eligibility by parking its eligibility in particular spots that the bidder is not interested in and then moves to its true interest later.
- The simultaneous ascending auction is typically done without package bids. The bidders are bidding on individual lots and there is the possibility that a bidder will win some of the lots that it needs for its business plan, but not all. This exposure to winning less than what the bidder needs has adverse consequences on efficiency. Essentially the bidder has to guess. Either the bidder goes for it or not. When there are complementarities, this is a tough decision for the bidder to make. The bidder may make the wrong decision and win something it actually does not want.
- The lack of package bids also makes the simultaneous ascending auction vulnerable to hold up, which is basically a speculator stepping in and taking advantage of a bidder. For example say you are Verizon, a big bidder, and I am Mario Gabelli, owner of a $30 billion investment fund. Gabelli was a frequent participant in the FCC spectrum auctions until recently, when he was sued and paid a $130 million settlement in a fraud case brought against him, because he always claimed to be a very small business, and received a discount of between 25% and 40% for making such a claim, despite his $30 billion in assets and $1 billion in net worth. But anyway, Gabelli´s apparent strategy was to make it clear to the large bidders that it would be expensive to push him out of the way. As a result, the large bidders would let him win some desirable lots at low prices, and then he would turn around and sell them to the big players after the auction was over, and make some quick money. That is

the holdup strategy. It is easy to do and effective. Preventing resale would reduce this problem, but resale is desirable in a rapidly changing dynamic industry.

- There is limited substitution across licenses, which is something I am going to emphasize. You might think that it would be easy to arbitrage across the lots, but in fact that is not the case. Especially in a large country like the United States, where the FCC splits up the frequency bands in different ways, geographically, and you can only bid on individual lots, rather than packages.

As a result of all these factors, the bidding strategies are quite complicated, which is nice if you happen to be advising bidders on spectrum auctions, but is a problem if you are a bidder, because you have to learn how to engage in all this complex bidding.

5. The US AWS and 700 MHz Auctions

The difficulties in arbitraging across substitutes are best illustrated in the two most recent major auctions in the United States: AWS and 700 MHz.

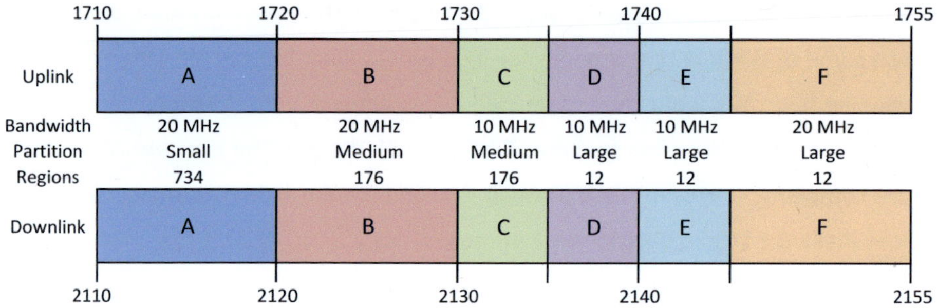

Figure 2: The US AWS band plan: something for everyone

First the AWS, Advances Wireless Services, auction sold 90 MHz of spectrum in 161 rounds, and raised 14 billion dollars. As in all of its auctions, the FCC began the process by settling on a specific band plan (the product design), which effectively determined how the available bandwidth in each location was going to be split up into lots, where each lot is a particular frequency band covering a particular geographic area. In the case of the AWS auction, the FCC decided that six frequency blocks of paired spectrum (A-F) were to be auctioned, as shown above. Three blocks were 20 MHz and three were 10 MHz. Because the US is so large, each frequency block was also partitioned geographically. And because the FCC was attempting to accommodate all types of bidders, the FCC partitioned the blocks in three different ways: for blocks D-F the country was split into 12 large regions; for blocks B and C the country was split into 176 medium-size regions; and for block A the country was split into 734 small regions. Remarkably, the different partitions do not form a hierarchy in the sense that you cannot construct one of the medium-sized lots by aggregating a number of small lots. This inability to aggregate small into medium clearly limits substitution across blocks.

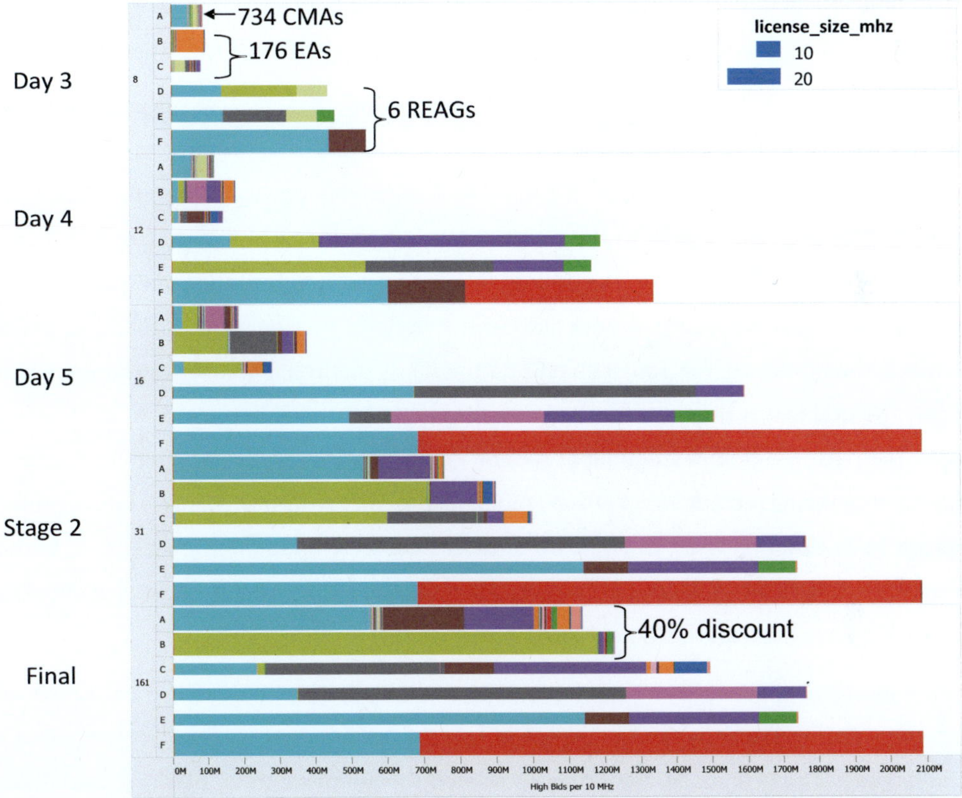

Sum of pwb amount per 10 MHz for each block broken down by round. Color shows details about pw_bidder. Size shows details about license_size_mhz. The view is filtered on pw_bidder and round. The pw_bidder filter excludes . The round filter keeps 8, 12, 16, 31 and 161

Figure 3: The absence of arbitrage across substitutes in the US AWS auction

The underlying substitution problem was caused both by the product design—the use of specific blocks following three different geographic schemes—and the auction format. Figure 3 illustrates the severe problems bidders had substituting across blocks in the AWS auction. It shows the price per 10 MHz of spectrum for each of the blocks at the end of critical days in the auction. Recall there are six blocks, so there are six bars (A through F) at the end of each day. The 20 MHz bars are twice as thick as the 10 MHz bars so the area of the bar corresponds to revenues at the time indicated. Finally, different colors represent different bidders, so you can see who the provisional winners are at the various times in the auction. The two largest bidders are T-Mobile (turquoise) and Verizon (red).

If there was perfect arbitrage across blocks, then what you would see is the length of the bars would be the same at each time in the auction, indicating equal prices across blocks. Over time, the prices would move higher, but the prices would tend to move together across the blocks, as bidders would arbitrage to the cheaper lots per MHz of spectrum.

What happened in the AWS auction is extremely far from that. Look at the end of day five. At this point, the F block has already reached its final price. The A block is less than one twentieth the price of the F block. If the A block is roughly equivalent to the F block, why wouldn't Verizon, say, switch to the much cheaper A block, instead of placing bids twenty times higher on the F block? The reason has to do with substitution difficulties. When Verizon is bumped off a large F block license, it is easy for Verizon to substitute down to the A block, submitting say the 100 or so bids on the A lots that roughly cover the corresponding F lot. The problem is that once shifting down it would be nearly impossible to shift back up to F. The reason is that in subsequent rounds Verizon would only be bumped from some of the corresponding A block lots. Verizon would have to withdraw from many A lots in order to return to F, exposing itself to large withdrawal penalties. In addition on block A, Verizon would be vulnerable to various hold-up strategies, where speculators could pick important holes in a synergistic aggregation of lots.

Since substituting down from large (F, E, D) to small (C, B, A) lots is easier than substituting up, the auction essentially proceeded in a sequential fashion. First, the bidders competed for the large-lot blocks (F, E, D), then they competed for the medium-lot blocks (C and B), and finally the competition fell to the small-lot block (A). This explains the sequential, rather than simultaneous price process across blocks.

Block	A	B	C
Bandwidth	12 MHz	12 MHz	22 MHz
Type	paired	paired	paired
Partition	176	734	12
Price	$1.16	$2.68	$0.76

Figure 4: Band plan and final prices ($/MHz-pop) for paired spectrum in 700 MHz auction

The next major auction in the US was the 700 MHz auction. The band plan for the paired spectrum is shown above. The FCC did the same thing in this auction. Specific blocks were auctioned, using three different partitions of the US. Again the different partitions did not form a hierarchy. The final prices per MHz-pop range from $0.76 for the C block to $2.68 for the B block. These final prices differ by over a factor of three. We see again that the substitution across blocks is far from perfect. Interestingly, this time it is the small-lot block B that sold for a high price, and the large-lot block C that sold for a low price—just the opposite of what happened in the AWS auction.

Although the C-block had an open access provision, requiring that the operator not discriminate against either devices or applications, the terms of open access were sufficiently watered down that I doubt it had much of an impact on the C-block price. In my view, the price difference was because competing bidders thought that competing on the C-block against Verizon (or perhaps AT&T and Verizon) was sufficiently hopeless that it would be better to focus on the A and B blocks.

The conclusion from the now long history of spectrum auctions using the simultaneous ascending auction is that it works reasonably well in simple situations with a single geographic scheme. However in more complex settings, the approach leads to complex bidding strategies that complicate the auction and may undermine the efficient assignment of spectrum.

6. A Better Way: the Package Clock Auction

Fortunately, there is a better way. All that is needed is a number of complementary enhancements that ultimately simplify the bidding process, improve its efficiency, and greatly expand its power.

First, much of the game playing, such as tacit collusion and other bid signaling, can be eliminated with a shift to anonymous bids. In a package clock auction the round-by-round revelation of information is limited to aggregate measures of competition. Limiting round reports to prices and excess demand for each product gives the bidders the information needed to form expectations about likely prices and in resolving common value uncertainty, yet such reports do not allow the signaling strategies that support tacit collusion. Moreover, the streamlined report simplifies bidder decision-making and keeps the bidders focused on what is most relevant, the relationship between prices and aggregate demand.

In most instances, spectrum lots covering the same region in adjacent frequencies are nearly perfect substitutes. To a close approximation, the bidder simply cares about the quantity of spectrum in MHz it has in the region, rather than the exact frequency location. Moreover, to minimize interference problems bidders prefer contiguous spectrum within any region. Thus, it makes sense in the initial stage to auction generic spectrum. The stage determines the quantity of contiguous spectrum won in each region. In this stage the spectrum is treated as if it were a homogenous good within each region. This is an enormous simplification of what is being sold. The idea is to treat each MHz of spectrum within a geographic region and a particular frequency band as perfect substitutes. We let the auction resolve first the main question of how much spectrum in each region each winner gets and at what price, before the auction turns to the more subtle and less important question of the exact frequencies.

Of course, there are some auctions where the differences across frequencies are too great to allow this simplified treatment, for example because of major interference differences by frequency, as the result of incumbents with a right to stay in the particular band. In such cases, the specific spectrum lots can be auctioned from the start, but in most cases, it is desirable to auction generic spectrum first and then determine the specific assignment in a second stage.

The specific assignment stage is simplified, since it only involves winners in the generic stage. The number of specific assignments typically is limited to the number of ways that the winners can be ordered. Thus, if there are m winners there are m! different specific assignments. For example, an auction with four winners in a particular region would have $4! = 4\times3\times2 = 24$ different possible specific assignments. Assuming separability across regions, each of the four bidders would only need to express preferences among at most 24 different specific assignments. This number is reduced further if we assume that the bidder only cares about its own specific assignment and not the location of the other winners, as is commonly the case. Then for example with four winners of equal size, each winner would only need to express three preferences: the incremental value from the bidder's third-best specific assignment compared with its fourth-best, the incremental value from the bidder's second-best assignment compared with its third-best, and the incremental value from the bidder's first-best assignment compared with its second-best.

The use of generic lots, wherever possible, simplifies the auction, enhances substitution, and improves price discovery. Despite these advantages the FCC has chosen in each of its 72 auctions to sell specific lots. This is a common mistake in auction design. Interestingly, even in countries that recognized the advantages of selling generic lots, such as the German 3G auction, the generic lots were auctioned using a method for specific lots; that is, in the German 3G auction, even though the lots were perfect substitutes, the bidders bid on specific lots.

Once generic lots are adopted the next innovation becomes easier to see—the adoption of simple and powerful techniques that are well-suited to auctioning many divisible goods.

The first innovation is an improved product design, based on generic spectrum in each service area, accommodating multiple types of use.

The second innovation is the use of a simultaneous clock auction. This is a simplification of the simultaneous ascending auction. Each product has its own clock indicating its current price. Because of generic lots, each product may consist of multiple lots. In each round, the bidder is asked to indicate for each product the quantity of lots desired at the current price. At the end of the round, the auctioneer adds up the individual bids and reports the excess demand for each product. The price is then increased on any product with excess demand. This process is repeated until there is no excess demand on any product.

The two critical differences between the clock auction and the simultaneous ascending auction are 1) the bidder only answers demand queries, stating the quantities desired at the announced prices, and 2) there is no need to identify provisionally winning bidders at the end of every round.

The third innovation is more subtle, but extremely powerful. One can interpret the demand vector reported by each bidder in each round as a package bid. The bidder is saying, "At these prices, I want this package of lots." Taking this interpretation seriously yields a combinatorial auction (or package auction) without the need for any optimization. This allows bidders to express complementarities within a simple price discovery process.

Larry Ausubel and I have been conducting exactly this sort of package auction since 2001 for electricity and gas products in France, Germany, Belgium, Denmark, Spain, Hungary, and the United States. Thus, far we have conducted over 60 high-stakes auctions with this format for assets worth about $10 billion. We also used the approach in a spectrum auction in Trinidad and Tobago in 2005. The approach has been highly successful.

The clock auction may end with some products in excess supply, as a result of complementarities among lots. In addition, since the clock process follows a single price path and only includes a limited number of price points, it is desirable to allow the bidder to specify additional bids in a supplementary round following the clock stage. The purpose is to let the bidder express preferences for additional packages that were missed by the clock process. In addition, the bidder can improve its bids on packages already bid on in the clock stage.

Once the clock bids and the supplementary bids are collected, an optimization is run to determine the value-maximizing generic assignment and prices. This two-step process of a clock auction followed by supplementary bids, which I call a package clock auction, was proposed by Larry Ausubel, Paul Milgrom, and me for spectrum auctions at an FCC auction conference in 2003. We proposed the same approach for spectrum auctions in the UK in 2006, as well as for airport takeoff and landing rights in 2003. Meanwhile, David Porter, Stephen Rassenti, Anil Roopnarine, and Vernon Smith demonstrated in the experimental lab the high efficiency of the approach in 2003.

Two critical elements of a successful package clock auction are the pricing rule and the activity rule. I will discuss both at length. These two important rules work together to ensure that the bids are an accurate expression of bidder preferences throughout the entire auction. The high efficiency of the package clock auction derives mainly from incentives for nearly truthful bidding. A pricing rule based on second pricing encourages truthful bidding; whereas, the activity rule based on revealed preference ensures that these incentives for truthful bidding are felt throughout the clock stage.

7. UK Spectrum Auctions

The need for a technology neutral auction is commonplace in today's world of rapidly developing communications technologies and applications. While the regulator can typically identify the viable candidate technologies based on early development, the regulator cannot decide how available spectrum should be split among the technologies without a market test. Examples are numerous, and several will be discussed here.

Ofcom, the independent regulator and competition authority for the UK communications industries, was the first to recognize and act on this need for a technology neutral auction. In spring 2006, Larry Ausubel and I proposed to Ofcom a version of the package clock auction. Since June 2006, I have been working with Ofcom in developing, testing, and implementing the design for a number of its auctions. Two such auctions, the 10-40 GHz auction and the L-band auction have occurred already. Both went very well, and provided a useful field test for the economically much larger 2.6 GHz auction scheduled to take place in the second-half of 2009. The Netherlands has also adopted this approach for its 2.6 GHz auction. Finally, Ofcom has proposed to use the package clock auction for the digital dividend auction to take place in 2010. The initial proposal presents some computational challenges given the quantity of spectrum and the number of technologies that are competing for that spectrum, although I suspect that some simplifications will be made as the range of possibilities narrows as we get closer to the auction date.

Ofcom has three main goals for the auction design. The auction should be technology neutral, allowing alternative viable technologies to compete for the spectrum on an equal basis. The auction should accommodate flexible spectrum usage rights, permitting the user to decide how the spectrum would be used, subject to minimizing interference externalities with neighbors. And the auction should promote an efficient assignment of the spectrum, putting the spectrum to its best use.

Simplicity and transparency are important secondary objectives. On simplicity, Ofcom recognized that satisfying the main objectives posed serious challenges, which could not be addressed with an auction design that is too simple. Moreover, simplicity has to be assessed recognizing the complexity of bidder participation. For example, the simultaneous ascending auction has simple rules, but incredibly complicated bidding strategies. In contrast, the package clock auction has more complex rules, but the rules have been carefully constructed to make participation especially easy. For the most part, the bidder can focus simply on determining its true preferences for packages it can realistically expect to win. In a package clock auction it is the auctioneer that needs to do the complex optimization, whereas the bidders can focus on their values for realistic packages.

Revenue maximization was explicitly excluded as an objective. Nonetheless, an efficient auction necessarily will generate substantial revenues. Indeed, my advice to countries is to focus on efficiency. A focus on revenues is short-sighted. In my view, the government is better off finding as much spectrum as possible and then auctioning it so as to put the spectrum to its best use. This approach creates a competitive and innovative market for communications, which has substantial positive spillovers to the rest of the economy. Under this approach, long-term revenues likely will far exceed those that would come from the maximization of short-term auction revenues.

8. The UK 2.6 GHz Auction

The UK 2.6 GHz auction illustrates well the benefit of the package clock auction. This auction is for 190 MHz of spectrum at frequencies (2.6 GHz) that make it especially well-suited for mobile broadband communications. Currently, there are two fourth-generation (4G) technologies competing worldwide to be the next standard for broadband wireless communications: LTE, which uses paired spectrum, and WiMAX, which uses unpaired spectrum. Both technologies work well with a lot size of 5 MHz, but LTE requires that the lots come is pairs, one for uplink and another for downlink. In addition, a 5 MHz guard band is required between the paired and unpaired use, as well as between any two competing unpaired operators.

Type	Paired (FDD uplink)														Unpaired (TDD)										Paired (FDD downlink)													
Lot	1	2	3	4	5	6	7	8	9	10	11	12	13	14	1	2	3	4	5	6	7	8	9	10	1	2	3	4	5	6	7	8	9	10	11	12	13	14
Frequency	2500	2505	2510	2515	2520	2525	2530	2535	2540	2545	2550	2555	2560	2565	2570	2575	2580	2585	2590	2595	2600	2605	2610	2615	2620	2625	2630	2635	2640	2645	2650	2655	2660	2665	2670	2675	2680	2685

Figure 5: CEPT band plan from Electronic Communications Committee Decision (05)05

Confronted with this setting, the European Commission decided in 2005 that the band plan should be as shown in Figure 5 with 140 MHz of spectrum set aside for paired use and the remaining 50 MHz for unpaired use. Each 2×5 MHz paired lot would consist of an uplink on the lower block and a downlink on the upper block with 120 MHz separation between the two. This is an example of a specific band plan. If Ofcom adopted this plan, they would foreclose other possibilities that may put the spectrum to better use. In particular, the Commission had no way to know that splitting the spectrum 140 MHz paired and 50 MHz unpaired is best. Perhaps an alternative band plan with 100 MHz of paired as shown in Figure 6 would be better.

Type	Paired (FDD uplink)										Unpaired (TDD)														Paired (FDD downlink)										Unpaired			
Lot	1	2	3	4	5	6	7	8	9	10	1	2	3	4	5	6	7	8	9	10	11	12	13	14	1	2	3	4	5	6	7	8	9	10	15	16	17	18
Frequency	2500	2505	2510	2515	2520	2525	2530	2535	2540	2545	2550	2555	2560	2565	2570	2575	2580	2585	2590	2595	2600	2605	2610	2615	2620	2625	2630	2635	2640	2645	2650	2655	2660	2665	2670	2675	2680	2685

Figure 6: Increase in unpaired spectrum maintaining 120 MHz duplex spacing

Or perhaps the future of WiMAX is so bright that all of the spectrum should be unpaired as shown in Figure 7.

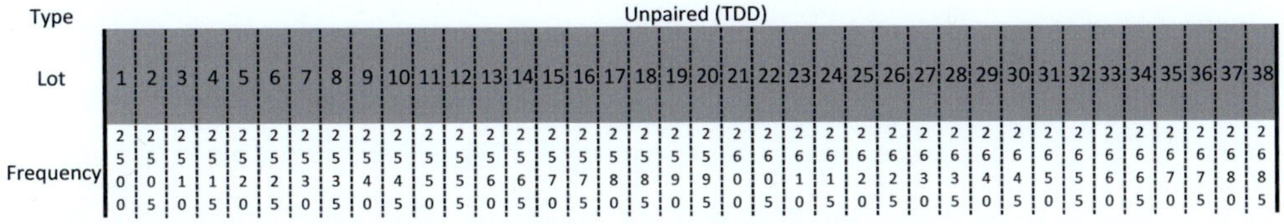

Figure 7: All unpaired spectrum

Fortunately, a package clock auction can resolve the question of the best band plan at the same time that spectrum winners are identified and the spectrum is priced. There is no reason that the regulator needs to specify the band plan; the auction can do that based on the competitive bids of the operators. Indeed, this can be an accomplished with an auction that is much simpler for bidders than the simultaneous ascending auction.

Here is how it works. The 140 MHz is split into 38 lots, 5 MHz each. The lots are perfect substitutes, since they are generic. All bids are package bids, so there is no exposure problem.

In the clock stage, the bidder simply specifies how many paired lots and how many unpaired lots it desires at the current prices. Packages of paired lots are guaranteed to be contiguous, as are packages of unpaired lots. In order to achieve 120 MHz spacing, consistent with the EC decision, it is necessary to have a minimum of 9 unpaired lots plus one 5 MHz guard block between the paired and unpaired use. If demand for paired and unpaired spectrum is such that this minimum constraint is not binding, then the paired and unpaired prices are linked at 2-1: one 2x5 MHz paired lot is priced at two times an unpaired lot; otherwise, if as a result of the minimum constraint of 9 unpaired lots, the price of unpaired lots may be lower than the paired price per 5 MHz. Thus, the clock stage has at most two prices, the price for unpaired lots and the price for paired lots. So long as there is excess demand of lots the clock prices continue to increase. Indeed, the clock prices will continue to increase until the point that the demands are feasible, which means that the demands can be met with contiguous awards. Notice that the clock stage is much simpler than the simultaneous ascending auction.

Following the clock stage, the bidders submit supplementary bids. The supplementary bids are either improvements to clock bids or bids on additional packages that were not bid on in the clock stage. For unpaired bidders, these additional bids can include the possibility of an award split between the lower block of unpaired spectrum and an upper block, which would be necessary if more than 9 unpaired lots are awarded.

Once the clock and supplementary bids are collected, the auction system takes all these bids and performs a series of optimizations to determine the value maximizing generic assignment, and the base prices to be paid by each winner.

The system also determines the feasible options each winner faces for specific assignments. These are reported to each winner, and the winner is asked to submit assignment bids indicating the incremental value derived from each option that is better than the winner's least preferred option. These assignment stage bids are then collected and another series of optimizations is performed to determine the value maximizing specific assignments and the additional payments the winners make in addition to the base prices calculated at the end of the supplementary round.

I now explain the details of two essential rules in the package clock auction: the pricing rule and the activity rule. The rules may appear complex, but the complexity actually simplifies the bidding strategies, making it easier for bidders to participate in the auction.

9. Pricing Rule: Closest-to-Vickrey Core Pricing

Prices are determined at two points in the auction, after the clock stage, including the supplementary bids, to determine the base prices for the winners in the value-maximizing generic assignment, and after the assignment stage to determine the additional payments for specific assignments.

The pricing rule plays a major role in fostering incentives for truthful bidding. Pay-as-bid pricing in a clock auction or a simultaneous ascending auction creates incentives for demand reduction. Large bidders shade their bids, recognizing their impact on price. This bid shading both complicates bidding strategies and also leads to inefficiency.

In contrast, Vickrey pricing provides ideal incentives for truthful bidding. Each winner pays the social opportunity cost of its winnings, and therefore receives 100 percent of the incremental value created by its bids. This aligns the maximization of social value with the maximization of individual value for every bidder. Thus, with private values, it is a dominant strategy to bid truthfully.

Unfortunately, as a result of complements, it may be that the Vickrey prices are too low in the sense that one or more bidders would be upset with the assignment and prices paid, claiming that they had offered the seller more. For example, suppose there are two items, A and B. Bidder 1 bids $4 for A, bidder 2 bids $4 for B, and bidder 3 bids $4 for A and B. The Vickrey outcome is for 1 to win A, 2 to win B, and each winner pays $0. Bidder 3 in this case has a legitimate complaint, "Why are you giving the goods to bidder 1 and 2, when I am offering $4 for the pair?" The basic problem is that with complements, the Vickrey outcome may not be in the core. Some coalition of bidders may have offered the seller more than the sum of the Vickrey prices. This point has been emphasized by Larry Ausubel and Paul Milgrom. (The core is defined as a set of payments that support the efficient assignment in the sense that there does not exist an alternative collation of bidders that has collectively offered the seller more.)

The solution is to increase one or more prices to assure that the prices are in the core. In order to provide the best incentives consistent with core pricing, we find the lowest payments that are in the core; that is, such that no alternative coalition of bidders has offered the seller more than the winning coalition is paying.

If we are auctioning a single item, then this is the second-price auction. Suppose the highest bidder bids $100 and the second-highest bidder bids $90. The item is awarded to the highest bidder, who pays the second-highest price of $90—the social opportunity cost of awarding the good to the highest bidder. Alternatively, we can think of assigning the item to maximize value, so we assign it to the highest bidder, and then we find the smallest payment that satisfies the core constraints. In this case, the second-highest bidder would be upset if the highest bidder paid less than $90, so $90 is the bidder-optimal core price. When the items are substitutes, then the bidder-optimal core point is unique and identical to the Vickrey prices.

Typically, the payment minimizing core prices, or bidder-optimal core prices, will not be unique. Thus, it will be important to have a method of selecting a unique bidder-optimal core point when there are many. The sensible approach adopted in each of the recent Ofcom auctions for both the base prices and the assignment prices is to select the payment minimizing core prices that are closest to the Vickrey prices. This is what I call closest-to-Vickrey core pricing. Since the set of core prices is convex—a polytope formed from the intersection of half-spaces—and the Vickrey prices are always unique, there is a unique vector of core prices that is closest in Euclidean distance to the Vickrey prices. Not only are the prices unique, but since they are bidder-optimal-core prices, they maximize the incentive for truthful bidding among all prices that satisfy core constraints.

The approach then is to take all the bids from the clock stage and the supplementary bids, determine the value maximizing assignment, and then determine the payment minimizing core prices that are closest to the Vickrey prices. It is my experience that bidders are quite happy with this approach—they like the idea of minimizing payments, and they recognize the importance of making sure that the prices are sufficiently high that no coalition of bidders has offered the seller more. Prices are as small as possible subject to all the competitive constraints.

Calculating the winning assignments and prices involves solving a sequence of standard optimization problems. The basic problem is the winner determination problem, which is a well understood set-packing problem. The main winner determination problem is to find the value maximizing assignment. To guarantee uniqueness, there is a sequence of lexicographic objectives, such as: 1) maximize total value, 2) minimize concentration, 3) maximize quantity sold, and 4) random. Thus, first you maximize total value. Then you add a constraint that the value equals this maximum value and you minimize concentration. Then you add another constraint that the concentration equals this minimum concentration and you maximize the quantity sold. Finally, you add a constraint that the quantity sold equals this maximum quantity and you maximize an objective based on random values for each bid rather than the true bids and resolve the optimization. This guarantees uniqueness.

Calculating the prices is a bit more involved. First, we determine the Vickrey prices by solving a sequence of winner determination problems, essentially removing one winner at a time to determine each winner's social opportunity cost of winning its package. Then we determine the bidder-optimal core prices using a clever constraint generation method proposed by Robert Day and S. Raghavan. Having found the Vickrey prices, we solve another optimization to find the most violated core constraint. If there is none, then we are done, since the Vickrey prices are in the core. Otherwise, we add this most-violated constraint and resolve the optimization, again finding the most violated core constraint. We add it to the optimization and re-solve. We keep doing this until there is no violated core constraint, and then we are done.

The reason that that Day-Raghavan approach is a highly efficient method of solution is because in practice there are typically only a handful of violated core constraints; thus, the procedure stops after just a few steps. In contrast the number of core constraints grows exponentially with the number of bidders and that makes including all the core constraints explicitly an inefficient method of solving the problem, both in time and memory.

As mentioned, the tie-breaking rule for prices is going to be important, since typically ties will arise along the southwest face of the core polytope. Finding the prices that are closest to the Vickrey prices involves solving a simple quadratic optimization. This gives us a unique set of prices. Uniqueness is important; it means that there is no discretion in identifying the outcome, either in the assignment or the prices.

An example will help illustrate all of these concepts. Suppose there are five bidders, 1, 2, 3, 4, 5, bidding for two lots, A and B. The following bids are submitted:

$b_1\{A\} = 28$

$b_2\{B\} = 20$

$b_3\{AB\} = 32$

$b_4\{A\} = 14$

$b_5\{B\} = 12$

Bidders 1 and 4 are interested in A, bidders 2 and 5 are interested in B, and bidder 3 is interested in the package A and B.

Determining the value maximizing assignment is easy in this example. Bidder 1 gets A and bidder 2 gets B, generating 48 in total value. No other assignment yields as much. Vickrey prices are also easy to calculate. If we remove bidder 1, then the best assignment gives A to bidder 4 and B to bidder 2, resulting in 34, which is better than the alternative of awarding both A and B to bidder 3, which yields 32. Thus, the social opportunity cost of bidder 1 winning A is 34 – 20 = 14 (the value lost from bidder 4 in this case). Similarly, if we remove bidder 2, then the efficient assignment is for bidder 1 to get A and bidder 5 to get B, resulting in 40. Then the social opportunity cost of bidder 2 winning B is 40 – 28 = 12 (the value lost from bidder 5). Hence, the Vickrey outcome is for bidder 1 to pay 14 for A and for bidder 2 to pay 12 for B. Total revenues are 14 + 12 = 26. Notice that bidder 3 has cause for complaint, since bidder 3 offered 32 for both A and B.

Now consider the core for this example. The core is represented in the payment space of the winning bidders—in this case the payments of bidders 1 and 2. Each bid defines a half-space of the payment space:

- Bidder 1's bid of 28 for A implies 1 cannot pay more than 28 for A.
- Bidder 2's bid of 20 for B implies 2 cannot pay more than 20 for B.

- Bidder 3's bid of 32 for AB implies that the sum of the payments for A and B must be at least 32.
- Bidder 4's bid of 14 for A implies that bidder 1 must pay at least 14 for A.
- Bidder 5's bid of 12 for B implies that bidder 2 must pay at least 12 for B.

The core is the intersection of these half-spaces as shown in Figure 8.

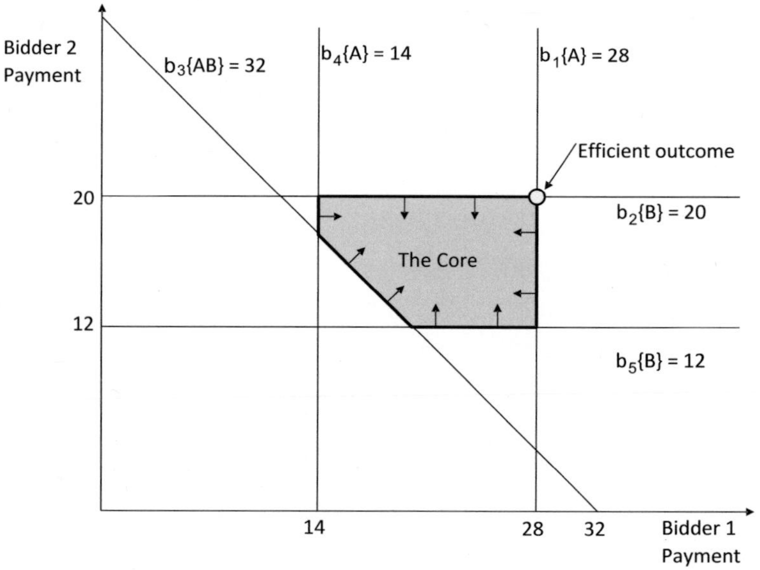

Figure 8: The Core

This example is quite general. First, unlike in some economic settings, in an auction, the core is always nonempty. The reason is that the core always includes the efficient outcome. The reason is that all the constraints are southwest of the efficient point, since the efficient point maximizes total value. Second, the core is always a convex polytope, since it is the intersection of numerous half-spaces. Third, complementarities, like bidder 3's bid for AB, are the source of the constraints that are neither vertical nor horizontal. These are the constraints that can put the Vickrey prices outside the core. Without complementarities, all the constraints will be vertical and horizontal lines, and there will be a unique extreme point to the southwest: the Vickrey prices.

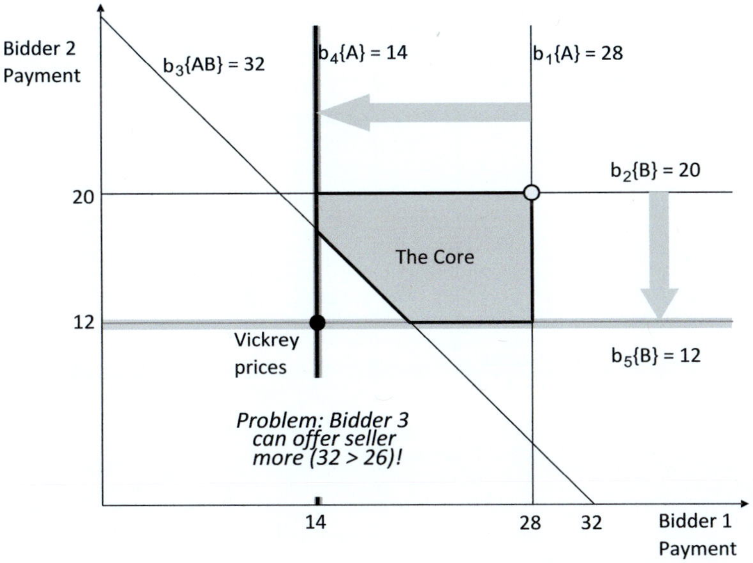

Figure 9: Vickrey prices: how much can each winner's bid be reduced holding others fixed?

The graphical representation of the core is also a useful way to see the Vickrey prices. Vickrey is asking how much can each winner unilaterally reduce its bids and still remain a winner. As shown in Figure 9, bidder 1 can reduce its bid to 14 before bidder 1 is displaced by bidder 4 as a winner. Similarly, bidder 2 can reduce its bid to 12 before being displaced by bidder 5. Thus, the Vickrey prices are 14 and 12. The problem is that these payments sum to 26, which violates the core constraint coming from bidder 3's bid of 32 for AB.

Bidder-optimal core prices can also be thought of maximal reductions in the bids of winners, but rather than reducing the bids of each winner one at a time, we jointly reduce all the winning bids, as shown in Figure 10, until the southwest face of the core is reached. As can be seen, this does not result in a unique core point, since the particular point on the southwest face depends on the rate at which each winner's bids are reduced. The bidder-optimal core points consist of the entire southwest face of the core. If the southwest face is a unique point, then it is the Vickrey prices; if the southwest face is not unique then the face is a core constraint involving complementarities, and the Vickrey prices lie outside the core.

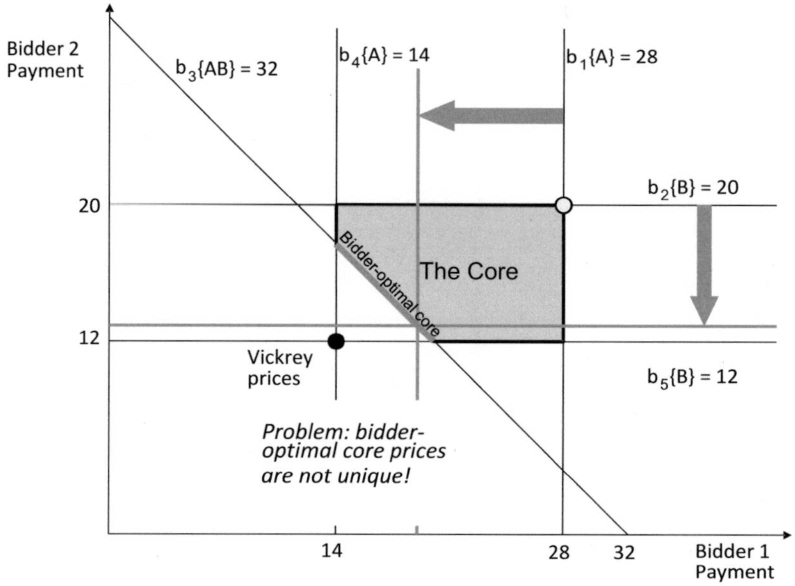

Figure 10: Bidder-optimal core prices: jointly reduce winning bids as much as possible

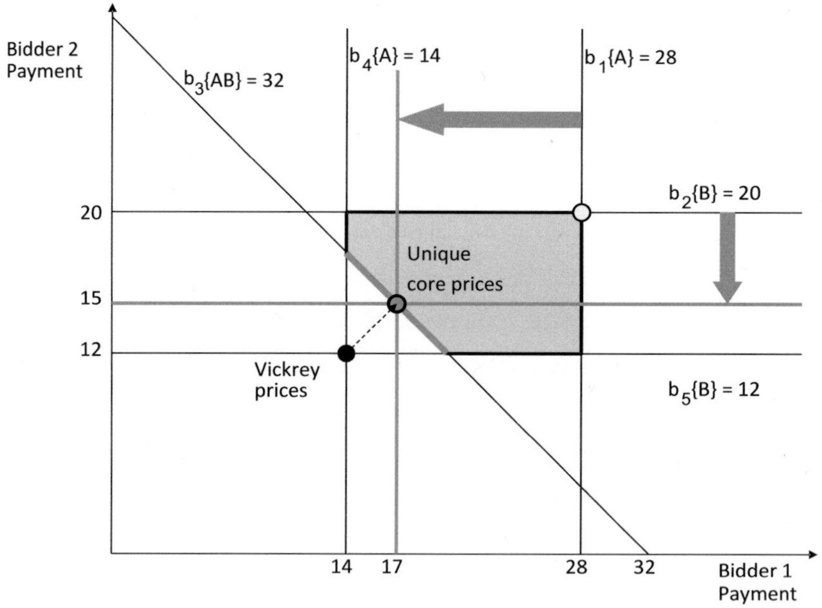

Figure 11: Core point closest to Vickrey prices

Nonetheless, there is always a unique core point that is closest to the Vickrey prices. This is seen in Figure 11, as the bidder-optimal core point that forms a 90 degree angle with the line that passes through the Vickrey prices. This point minimizes the Euclidean distance from the Vickrey prices.

Closest-to-Vickrey core pricing was adopted in each of the UK spectrum auctions, both the two that have already been held as well as the proposed auctions for the 2.6 GHz spectrum and the digital dividend spectrum. Closest-to-Vickrey core pricing is also proposed in the Netherlands 2.6 GHz auction, and in the US auction for takeoff and landing slots at the New York City airports.

Bidder-optimal core pricing has several advantages. First, it minimizes the bidders' incentive to distort bids in a Pareto sense: there is no other pricing rule that provides strictly better incentives for truthful bidding. Bidder-optimal core pricing implies Vickrey pricing, whenever Vickrey is in the core. For example, when lots are substitutes, Vickrey is in the core, and the bidders have an incentive to bid truthfully. Since the prices are in the core, it avoids the problem of Vickrey prices being too low as a result of complements. Finally, the rule has the desirable property that revenue is monotonic in bids and bidders. Adding either bids or bidders can only increase revenues. In contrast, Vickrey prices, as a result of complements, can either increase or decrease as either bids or bidders are added.

10. Activity Rule: Simplified Revealed Preference

Good price discovery is essential in realizing the benefits of a dynamic auction. Good price discovery stems from providing incentives for the bidders to make truthful bids throughout the auction process. The pricing rule discussed in the prior section is one essential element, but you also have to be concerned about what we see on eBay every day: bid sniping—jumping in at the last instance in an auction, holding your information back and not revealing it to the market. Bid sniping is an effective strategy in eBay auctions, and is typically used by experienced eBay bidders. The strategy is made possible on eBay, because eBay does not have an activity rule. In contrast, nearly all high-stake auctions, such as the FCC spectrum auctions, do have an activity rule. The FCC uses a quantity-based rule. This rule has worked reasonably well in the FCC's simultaneous ascending auctions, but in a package clock auction with closest-to-Vickrey core pricing, we need a more complex rule, one that is based on revealed preference. A rule based on revealed preference is effective at getting bidders to focus on their valuations and to bid in a profit maximizing way throughout the auction.

Absent an activity rule, bidders will have an incentive to hold back to conceal information. This bid sniping behavior is so common in eBay auctions that the auctions are better modeled as sealed-bid second-price auctions, rather than ascending auctions. The activity rule is intended to promote truthful bidding throughout the auction process. An effective activity rule will enhance price discovery, enabling the bidders to better focus on relevant packages and to resolve common-value uncertainty.

As mentioned, the traditional activity rule in both simultaneous ascending auctions and clock auctions has been a quantity-based rule: to be a large winner at the end of the auction, the bidder must be a large bidder throughout the auction. In particular, each lot corresponds to a particular quantity of spectrum, measured in either MHz-pop (the bandwidth times the population) or in eligibility points. The bidder starts with an initial eligibility based on the bidder's initial deposit. To maintain this level of eligibility in future rounds, the bidder needs to bid on a sufficiently large quantity of spectrum in the current round, where "sufficiently large" is stated as some percentage, typically between 80% and 100% of the bidder's current eligibility. If the bidder bids on a smaller quantity, the bidder's eligibility is reduced in future rounds. This quantity-based rule has worked reasonably well, although as mentioned, it does create an incentive for parking eligibility on lots that a bidder is not truly interested in, especially if the eligibility points are not a good measure of relative value across lots. (The FCC's MHz-pop measure is especially poor with small lots. Spectrum in New York City is much scarcer than spectrum in Montana. As a result, spectrum prices (and values) are much higher in New York City on a per MHz-pop basis. Despite this obvious fact, demonstrated in many dozens of spectrum auctions, the FCC still continues to use MHz-pop as the quantity measure in its auctions, exacerbating parking and other problems associated with the activity rule.)

In many clock auctions, an activity requirement of 100% is used, which means that the bidder cannot increase the size of the package, as measured in eligibility points, as prices rise. For the case of a single product, this means that the bidder must bid in a manner consistent with a downward-sloping demand curve.

In a package clock auction, one can use this quantity-based rule in the clock stage, but one also needs to specify how the rule limits bids in the supplementary round. This linkage between the clock bids and the supplementary bids is of critical importance, for otherwise the bidder could bid snipe, submitting all of its bids in the supplementary round.

Ofcom proposed the following, which I call the *eligibility point rule*. During the clock stage, the bidder cannot increase the package size. Moreover, whenever the bidder reduces the package size, the bid on all larger packages is capped by the prices at the time of the reduction. For example, if during the clock stage a bidder drops from a package of size 10 to 6 at prices p, then for all packages q of size 7 to 10, the supplementary bid cannot be more than $p \cdot q$.

The eligibility point rule, which Ofcom used in its first two package clock auctions, has the advantage of simplicity. For each package there is at most a single linear constraint on the supplementary bid. However, it has a potentially serious problem. The straightforward strategy of bidding on the most profitable package in the clock stage is a poor strategy. A bidder following such a strategy would find that its supplementary bids would be sharply constrained, well below true values. To avoid this problem, the bidder must instead bid in the clock stage to maximize package size, subject to a nonnegative profit constraint. That is, the bidder throughout the clock stage bids on the largest package that is still profitable.

Larry Ausubel, Paul Milgrom, and I proposed an alternative activity rule based on revealed preference for the package clock auction. Revealed preference is the underlying motivation for all activity rules. We wish to require that a bidder bid in a way throughout the auction that is consistent with the bidder's true preferences. Since we do not know the bidders true preferences, the best we can hope for is for the bidder to bid in a manner that is consistent with its revealed preferences. In the simplest case of a single-product clock auction, this is equivalent to monotonicity in quantity, just like the eligibility point rule, but when we have multiple products the two rules differ in important ways.

For the package clock auction, the *revealed preference rule* is as follows. During the clock stage, a bidder can only shift to packages that have become relatively cheaper; that is, at time $t' > t$, package $q_{t'}$ has become relatively cheaper than q_{t+}:

(P) $$q_{t'} \cdot (p_{t'} - p_t) \leq q_t \cdot (p_{t'} - p_t).$$

Moreover, every supplementary bid $b(q)$ must be less profitable than the revised package bid $b(q_t)$ at t:

(S) $$b(q) \leq b(q_t) + (q - q_t) \cdot p_t.$$

That is, each clock bid for package q_t, as improved in the supplementary round, imposes a cap on the supplementary bid for package *q*.

An important advantage of the revealed preference rule is that a bidder following the straightforward strategy of bidding on its most profitable package in the clock stage would retain the flexibility to bid its full value on all packages in the supplementary round.

To illustrate the implications of the two activity rules, consider the following example with two bidders and two identical lots (one product) in a setting of substitutes. The bidders' preferences are given in the table below, indicating the marginal and average value for 1 lot and 2 lots.

	Marginal Value		Average Value	
	Bidder A	Bidder B	Bidder A	Bidder B
1 lot	16	8	16	8
2 lots	2	2	9	5

Since the lots are substitutes, both bidders want to bid their true values in the supplementary round. However, consider what happens in the clock stage in response to the two different rules.

With the revealed preference rule, each bidder has an incentive to bid on its most profitable package in each round. Thus, the bidding simply moves up each bidder's marginal value (demand) curve. When the clock price reaches 2, both bidders drop from a package of size 2 to 1, and excess demand drops to zero. The clock stage ends at the competitive equilibrium price of 2 and the efficient assignment. Indeed, there is no need for any supplementary bids in this case. Bidder A can enter supplementary bids of 16 and 18, and bidder B can enter supplementary bids of 8 and 10, but these supplementary bids will not change the outcome in any way. Each bidder wins one lot and pays 2 (the Vickrey price). The supplementary round is unnecessary. The clock stage, by revealing the bidders marginal value information, up to the point of no excess demand, has revealed all that is needed to determine and price the efficient assignment. This is a general result with substitutes.

With the eligibility point rule, bidders are forced to distort their bidding away from the straightforward strategy of profit maximization. In order to preserve the ability to bid full values in the supplementary round, the bidders instead bid on the largest package that is still profitable. This entails moving up the average value curve, since when the average value is exceeded a package is no longer profitable. Thus, when the clock price reaches 5, bidder B's average value for 2 is reached and the bidder drops its demand to 1. Then when the clock price reaches 8, bidder B's average value for 1 is reached and bidder B drops out. At this point there is no excess demand, so the clock stage ends with bidder A demanding 2, bidder B demanding zero, and the clock price at 8. In the supplementary bid round, the bidders again submit their true preferences, and the optimization determines that each bidder should win one lot and should pay 2. The supplementary round was required to determine the efficient assignment and price the goods. Notice that the clock stage did little but mislead the bidders into thinking that bidder A would win all the items at a high price.

The reader might think that I somehow rigged this example to make the eligibility point rule look bad. This is not the case. Whenever lots are substitutes, the same features will be observed. With revealed preference, the clock stage will converge to the competitive equilibrium, revealing the efficient outcome and supporting prices; whereas with the eligibility point rule, the clock stage ends with an assignment that is excessively concentrated and prices that are too high. This result follows from the simple fact that average value exceeds marginal value, whenever aggregate demand is downward sloping, as shown in Figure 12. Having participated in many dozens of major spectrum auctions, I can confirm that this is indeed the typical case.

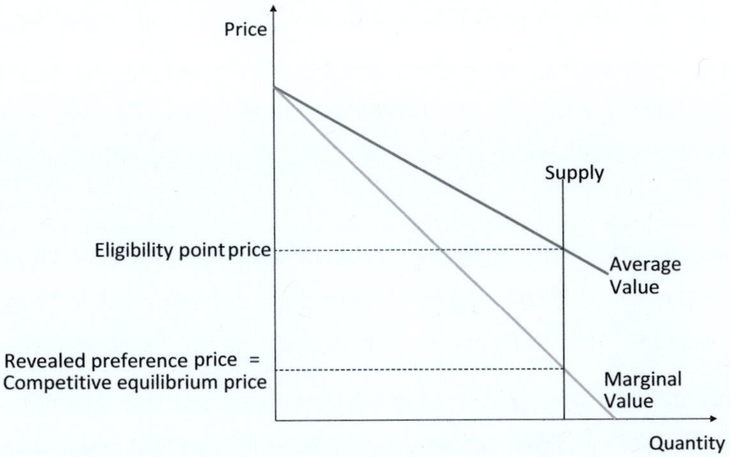

Figure 12: Downward sloping aggregate demand implies average value > marginal value

In Figure 13, I show another example with a supply of 18 identical lots and five bidders, each with a different constant elasticity of demand. Marginal values are shown in the first five columns and average values are shown in the next five. The clock stage with the revealed preference rule is shown in green. The bidders bid to maximize profit and so reduce demands as marginal values are reached. The clock stage ends at a price of 370, the competitive equilibrium price and the assignment is efficient.

Weaker bidder reveals too much

	Demand Elasticity									
	0.50	0.60	0.70	0.80	0.90					
	Marginal Value					Average Value				
Lots	Bidder A	Bidder B	Bidder C	Bidder D	Bidder E	Bidder A	Bidder B	Bidder C	Bidder D	Bidder E
1	10,000	4,642	2,683	1,778	1,292	10,000	4,642	2,683	1,778	1,292
2	2,500	1,462	997	748	598	6,250	3,052	1,840	1,263	945
3	1,111	744	558	450	381	4,537	2,282	1,413	992	757
4	625	461	370	314	277	3,559	1,827	1,152	823	637
5	400	317	269	238	216	2,927	1,525	975	706	553
6	278	234	207	189	176	2,486	1,310	847	620	490
7	204	181	166	156	149	2,160	1,149	750	553	441
8	156	145	138	132	128	1,909	1,023	674	501	402

Too concentrated

Bidding norm	Clearing Price					Total Value
Max profit	370		Supply	18	Max profit	31,428
Max size	1,292	Price too high	Misassigned	5	Max size	29,150
Difference	249%		Fraction misassigned	28%	Inefficiency	7.3%

Figure 13: An example with five bidders and constant demand elasticity

In contrast, with the eligibility point rule, the outcome is shown in yellow. The clock stage outcome is too concentrated, misassigning 5 of the 18 lots and causing an inefficiency of 7.3%. The final price is 2.5 times the competitive equilibrium. The rule also forces the weakest bidder to reveal its entire demand schedule; whereas the strongest bidder reveals nothing.

What is essential for price discovery is the revelation of the marginal value information. This helps bidders make the marginal tradeoffs that are of greatest relevance in figuring out what the outcome should be. This is why I believe the eligibility point rule is a poor choice.

To further test the two activity rules, I conducted numerous simulations using realistic demand scenarios with significant complementarities from both technological and minimum scale constraints. I assumed that the bidders bid on the most profitable package with revealed preference (max profit) and bid on the largest profitable package with the eligibility point rule (max size). The results are summarized in Figure 14. Notice how the revealed preference rule achieves substantially higher efficiency in many fewer rounds.

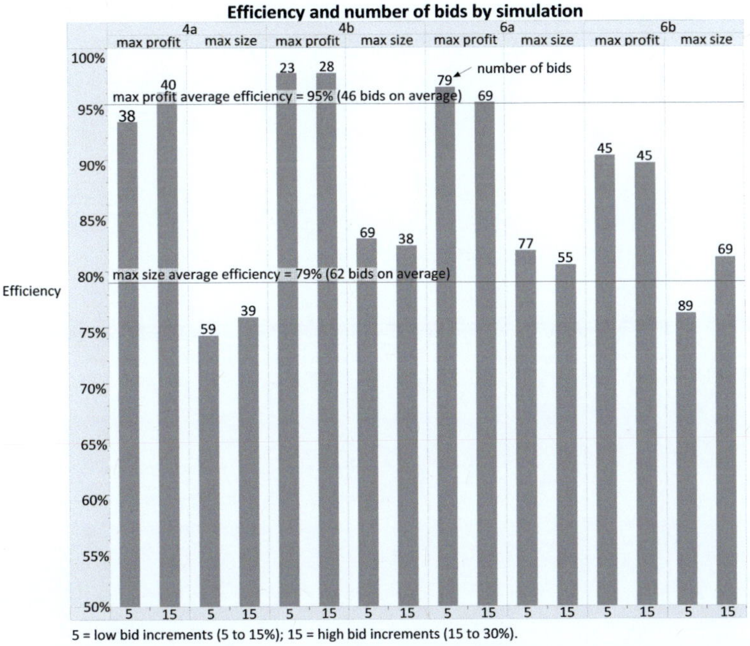

Figure 14: Revealed preference rule yields higher efficiency and fewer bids in the clock stage

Figure 15 shows the better price discovery of the revealed preference rule as observed in the simulations. The top-two rows show the price path with a minimum bid increment of 5% under the revealed preference rule and the eligibility point rule, respectively. Notice the tendency for the price path under max-size bidding to go up too quickly and overshoot the competitive equilibrium price, creating excess supply (in red). The bottom two rows show the same scenarios, but with a larger minimum bid increment of 15%.

As a final test of the two activity rules, as well as other elements of the auction design, I conducted a series of full-scale tests in the experimental lab. For the tests, the Ofcom auction platform was used and indeed Ofcom staff served as the auctioneer. The subjects in the test were PhD students, who had taken an advanced course in game theory and auction theory, and had prior participation in package clock auction experiments. I chose such an experienced and expert subject pool, since in the actual spectrum auctions bidders often hire experts and devote substantial time and money to understand the strategic implications of the rules.

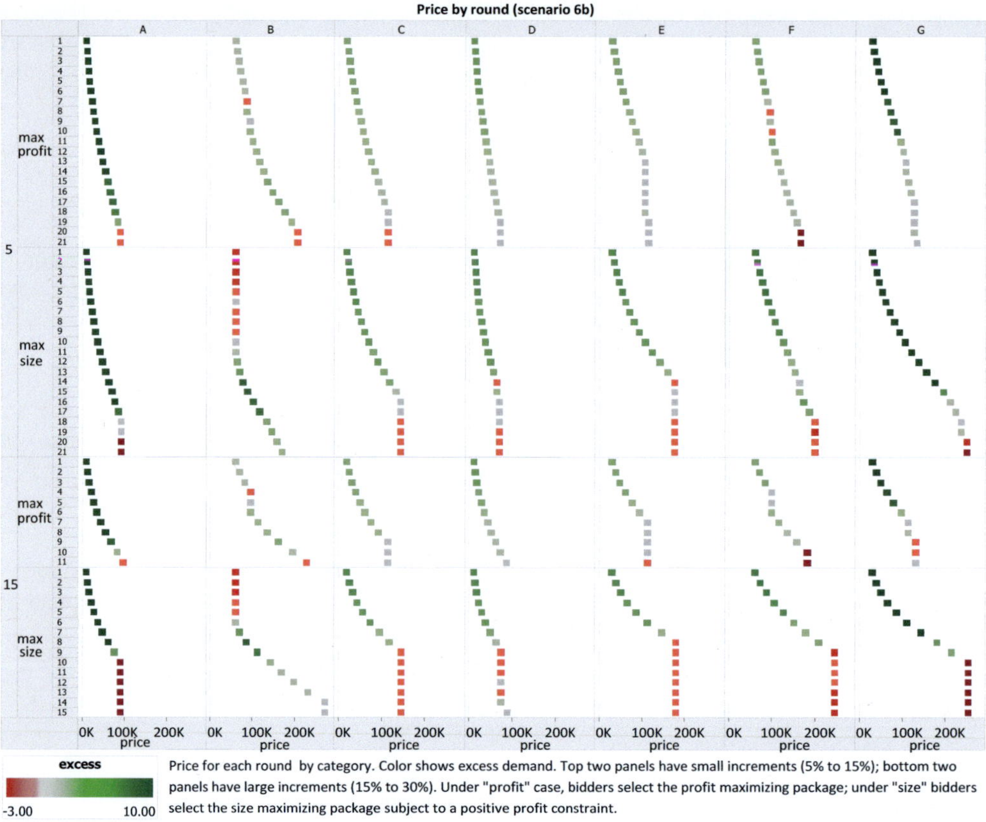

Price for each round by category. Color shows excess demand. Top two panels have small increments (5% to 15%); bottom two panels have large increments (15% to 30%). Under "profit" case, bidders select the profit maximizing package; under "size" bidders select the size maximizing package subject to a positive profit constraint.

Figure 15: Price path for revealed preference and eligibility point rules by product

Each subject participated in several auctions over a two-week period. In each auction, the subject was given a bidding tool, which calculated the subject's value for each package consistent with the bidder's business plan. The scenarios as represented by the various bidding tools were chosen to be realistic. The valuation models included both substitutes and complements. Complements came from minimum scale constraints as well as technological requirements. A training session was held before the auctions to explain the details of the package clock auction, including the two different activity rules. All subjects participated in both activity rule treatments. Each subject was paid an amount based on her experimental profits. The average subject payment was $420.

The experiments confirmed that the eligibility point rule caused a major deviation from straightforward bidding in the clock stage. Bidders quickly realized the need to bid on the largest profitable package. This undermined price discovery, but given the private value setting and simple valuation models, the poor performance of the clock stage was largely corrected by the supplementary bids and the optimization that followed. There were some instances of inefficiency when bidders deviated from bidding on the largest profitable package and then found they were unable to bid full values in the supplementary stage.

In contrast, with the revealed preference rule, bidders almost always followed the straightforward strategy of bidding on the most profitable package. In the supplementary round, bidders typically bid full value and were not constrained by the revealed preference rule. As a result, efficiency was nearly 100%.

One issue that was discovered in the lab was the complexity of the revealed preference rule. The few bidders who deviated from bidding on the most profitable package in each round of the clock stage found they were unable to bid full value in the supplementary round as a result of the revealed preference constraint. The difficulty for these bidders was that it was difficult for them to determine how high they could bid, since revealed preference is not a single constraint, but one constraint for each clock bid. Moreover, improving the bids on various clock packages causes the constraints to change. The challenge for the bidder is to figure out how best to adjust numerous bids in order to satisfy many constraints (one per round). Even the brightest PhD students found this to be a daunting task without some computational help.

One solution to the complexity problem is for the auction system to provide the bidder with some help. For example, the bidder could provide the system with its desired bids. The auction system then would indicate a summary of the bids that currently violate revealed preference constraints and suggest an alternative set of bids that satisfies all constraints and is closest (in Euclidean distance) to the desired bids. This is exactly the information the subjects in the lab were looking for in the few instances of deviations from straightforward bidding. In the lab, the deviations were minor and the bids would have been easily adjusted with the help of a smart auction system. The optimization I propose is a quadratic optimization with linear constraints. It is easily solved in an instant.

In addition to complexity, the revealed preference rule may at times be too strong. Bidders' values may change over the course of the auction for example as the result of common value uncertainty.

11. Simplifying Revealed Preference

A simplified revealed preference rule may address both the complexity and changing values issues. The idea behind the rule is that it may be unnecessary to include all of the revealed preference constraints to get the bidders to adopt the straightforward bidding. Since the incentive for bid sniping is not too strong, even the possibility of a revealed-preference constraint may be sufficient to induce the desired behavior. People put coins in parking meters in order to avoid the possibility of a parking ticket. We can hope that a simplified revealed preference rule will have the same effect in the package clock auction.

The *simplified revealed preference rule* imposes only a subset of revealed preference constraints. At most one revealed preference constraint applies to each bid. In the clock stage, the bidder can shift to any package of the same or smaller size without constraint. However, the bidder can only shift to larger packages that satisfy revealed preference with respect to the prior bid; that is, at time *t*, if package q_t is larger than package q_{t-1}, then q_t has become relatively cheaper than q_{t-1}:

(P′) $$q_{t'} \cdot (p_{t'} - p_t) \leq q_t \cdot (p_{t'} - p_t).$$

Moreover, all supplementary bids $b(q)$ are capped by a single revealed preference constraint. Packages q the same size or smaller than q_f are capped by revealed preference with respect to the final clock package q_f:

(S′) $$b(q) \leq b(q_f) + (q - q_f) \cdot p_f.$$

Packages q larger than q_f also must satisfy revealed preference with respect to the smaller package q_s (where round s is the first round a package smaller than q was bid for):

(S′′) $$b(q) \leq b(q_s) + (q - q_s) \cdot p_s.$$

Notice that all the constraints are revealed preference constraints, so this indeed is a simplified revealed preference rule. Also, notice that for each package, there is at most a single revealed preference constraint that limits the bid. Thus, conforming to the rule is a simple one-dimensional problem. Just as with the eligibility point rule, there is no need for optimization tools to help the bidder conform to the rule.

One of the desirable features of the rule is that the final package in the clock stage plays an especially important role in limiting bids on all packages that are not larger than the final package. Thus, any distortion from profit maximization in the final clock package is especially costly to the bidder. Of course, the bidder never knows, which clock round will be the last, so there is always some incentive to bid consistent with profit maximization. Moreover, as excess demand falls, the probability that the current round will be the last tends to increase, strengthening the incentive for straightforward bidding throughout the clock stage.

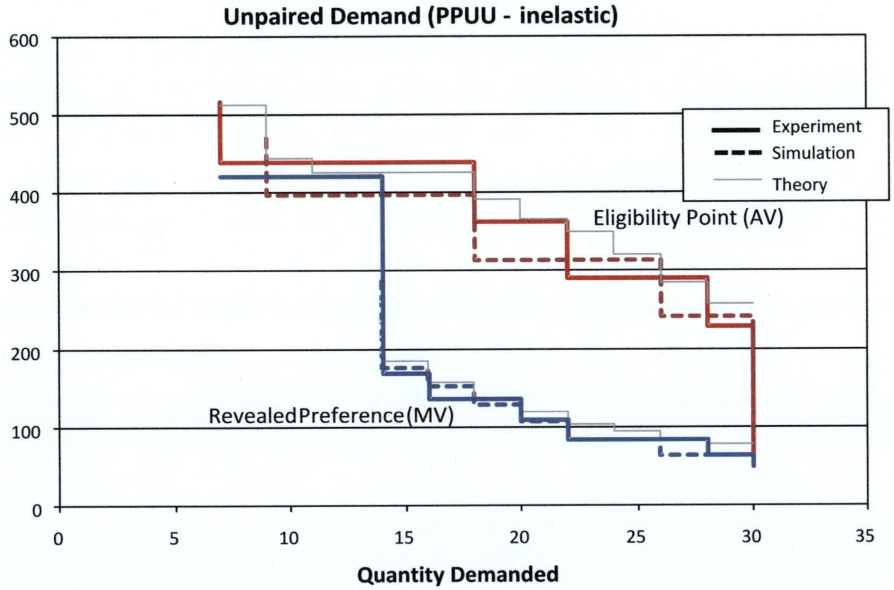

Figure 16: Comparison of theory, simulation, and experiment in the 2.6 GHz auction

I tested a version of the simplified revealed preference rule for the UK 2.6 GHz auction. The methodology was as in the earlier tests. First I developed a number of realistic scenarios. The two activity rules were then evaluated using a theoretical clock auction with continuous prices, a simulation with discrete increments, and then in the experimental lab with the same experienced PhD students that participated in the earlier tests. Figure 16 compares the demand curves as bid in the clock stage under the two activity rules for a typical scenario. The subjects bid in a manner consistent with the assumed behavior in both the theory and the simulation. From this I conclude that the simplified revealed preference rule has all of the desirable properties of the revealed preference rule, without the complexity.

Ofcom has adopted a version of the simplified revealed preference rule for the 2.6 GHz auction.

12. Challenges of the Digital Dividend

The 2.6 GHz auction is an especially simple application of the package clock auction. There are just two technologies (WiMAX and LTE) and they interact in an especially simple way.

The challenges of the digital dividend are much greater. At least currently, there are many competing technologies. In addition to WiMAX and LTE, mobile TV and digital terrestrial television are also possible. Moreover, there are many ways to break the spectrum up.

In 2008 the UK made one proposal for auctioning the digital dividend. The proposal was among the most complicated auction proposals ever made. The reason for the complexity is that Ofcom wants the auction to make the tough decisions about how to organize the spectrum based on the bids, rather than through regulatory dictate. Because the preliminary proposal was made so far in advance of the auction date, there was greater uncertainty about how much flexibility will ultimately be needed. My guess is that as we get closer to the auction date, more features will be resolved and as a result a simpler auction ultimately will be possible. Nonetheless, even in its most complex form, the complexity was on the auctioneer side, not on the bidder side. The original proposal would be entirely manageable for the bidders. This is a key feature of good auction design. The auction system, not the bidders, should do the heavy lifting in terms of optimization of bids; the bidders then can focus on valuing the assets and expressing preferences.

13. Conclusion

The package clock auction is a large advance over the standard simultaneous ascending auction. It eliminates the exposure problem, it eliminates most gaming behavior, it enhances substitution, and it encourages competition. Most importantly, the package clock auction enables a technology neutral auction, which should be especially important with respect to the digital dividend. The auction, through the competitive bids, determines how the spectrum is organized, rather than the regulator. In an environment where the regulator has only a rumor of an idea about what technology or use is best, letting the auction resolve such matters can greatly expand the realized value of the scarce spectrum resource.

A further advantage of the package clock auction is that it is readily customized for a variety of settings. Typically, a communications regulator will have a sequence of auctions over many years, as new spectrum gradually is made available. The package clock auction can be adapted to the unique characteristics of any particular auction. Adopting a consistent and flexible auction platform reduces transaction costs for the government and, more importantly, the bidders.

The auction design also enhances competition. The process is highly transparent and encourages price discovery. There is enhanced substitution both through the product design and the auction format. Bidder participation costs are reduced.

As in any market design problem, an important task for the regulator is to identify and mitigate potential market failures. In this setting and many others, the most important potential failure is market power. This is especially an issue in settings where there already is a highly concentrated communications market and the spectrum is an essential input for any new entrant. The approach here allows the regulator to address this potential market failure, as well as others, with a variety of instruments, such as spectrum caps, set asides, or bidding credits. The instruments must be used with care, or else they may do more harm than good.

One of the greatest harms is delaying the allocation and award of spectrum. Avoiding economic loss from delay should be a main priority of the regulator. Incumbents often will argue that spectrum awards should be put off. Such arguments may simply be a far less costly means of impeding competition than outbidding an entrant in an auction.

Fortunately, the use of a state-of-the-art auction design, such as the package clock auction and its variants, does not cause delay. These auctions can be designed and implemented, even by developing countries, in short order, provided the country is using successful techniques adopted elsewhere. The bottleneck is regulatory procedures, not auction design and implementation. Providers of auction services can readily meet deadlines of a few months if necessary.

The package clock auction can be applied in many other industries. For example, the approach was proposed and tested for the auctioning of takeoff and landing slots at New York City's airports. The approach is well-suited for any setting in which there are many interrelated items, some of which are substitutes and some of which are complements.

More broadly, the approach described here is an example of using auction design to harness the power of markets. The approach leads to improved pricing of a scarce resource, improving decision making, both short term and long term. Innovation is fostered from the better pricing and assignment of the scarce resource.

14. Acknowledgment

This talk largely is based on my paper, "Spectrum Auction Design." I thank my collaborators, Larry Ausubel, Robert Day, and Paul Milgrom for helpful discussions, as well as Nathaniel Higgins, Evan Kwerel, Thayer Morrill, Peter Pitsch, and Andrew Stocking. I thank the staff at Ofcom, especially Graham Louth, Director of Spectrum Markets, whose leadership and intellectual contribution were essential to the successful implementation of the package clock auction. I am grateful to the National Science Foundation and the Rockefeller Foundation for funding.

15. Suggestions for further reading

Ausubel, Lawrence M. (2004), "An Efficient Ascending-Bid Auction for Multiple Objects," *American Economic Review*, 94:5, 1452–1475.

Ausubel, Lawrence M. (2006), "An Efficient Dynamic Auction for Heterogeneous Commodities," *American Economic Review*, 96:3, 602–629.

Ausubel, Lawrence M. and Peter Cramton (2002), "Demand Reduction and Inefficiency in Multi-Unit Auctions," University of Maryland Working Paper 9607, revised July 2002.

Ausubel, Lawrence M. and Peter Cramton (2004), "Auctioning Many Divisible Goods," *Journal of the European Economic Association*, 2, 480–493, April-May.

Ausubel, Lawrence M., Peter Cramton, R. Preston McAfee, and John McMillan (1997), "Synergies in Wireless Telephony: Evidence from the Broadband PCS Auctions," *Journal of Economics and Management Strategy*, 6:3, 497–527.

Ausubel, Lawrence M., Peter Cramton, and Paul Milgrom (2006), "The Clock-Proxy Auction: A Practical Combinatorial Auction Design," in Peter Cramton, Yoav Shoham, and Richard Steinberg (eds.), *Combinatorial Auctions*, Chapter 5, 115–138, MIT Press.

Ausubel, Lawrence M. and Paul Milgrom (2002), "Ascending Auctions with Package Bidding," *Frontiers of Theoretical Economics*, 1:1, 1–45, www.bepress.com/bejte/frontiers/vol1/iss1/art1.

Ausubel, Lawrence M. and Paul Milgrom (2006a), "Ascending Proxy Auctions," in Peter Cramton, Yoav Shoham, and Richard Steinberg (eds.), *Combinatorial Auctions*, Chapter 3, 79–98, MIT Press.

Ausubel, Lawrence M. and Paul Milgrom (2006b), "The Lovely but Lonely Vickrey Auction," in Peter Cramton, Yoav Shoham, and Richard Steinberg (eds.), *Combinatorial Auctions*, Chapter 1, 17–40, MIT Press.

Brusco, Sandro and Giuseppe Lopomo (2002), "Collusion via Signalling in Simultaneous Ascending Bid Auctions with Heterogeneous Objects, with and without Complementarities," *Review of Economic Studies*, 69, 407–436.

Bulow, Jeremy, Jonathan Levin, and Paul Milgrom (2009), "Winning Play in Spectrum Auctions," Working Paper, Stanford University.

Coase, Ronald H. (1959), "The Federal Communications Commission," *Journal of Law and Economics*, 2, 1–40.

Cramton, Peter (1995), "Money Out of Thin Air: The Nationwide Narrowband PCS Auction," *Journal of Economics and Management Strategy*, 4, 267–343.

Cramton, Peter (1997), "The FCC Spectrum Auctions: An Early Assessment," *Journal of Economics and Management Strategy*, 6:3, 431–495.

Cramton, Peter (2006), "Simultaneous Ascending Auctions," in Peter Cramton, Yoav Shoham, and Richard Steinberg (eds.), *Combinatorial Auctions*, Chapter 4, 99–114, MIT Press.

Cramton, Peter, Evan Kwerel, and John Williams (1998), "Efficient Relocation of Spectrum Incumbents," *Journal of Law and Economics*, 41, 647–675.

Cramton, Peter and Jesse Schwartz (2002), "Collusive Bidding in the FCC Spectrum Auctions," *Contributions to Economic Analysis & Policy*, 1:1, www.bepress.com/bejeap/contributions/vol1/iss1/art11.

Cramton, Peter, Yoav Shoham, and Richard Steinberg (2006), *Combinatorial Auctions*, Cambridge, MA: MIT Press.

Cramton, Peter, Andrzej Skrzypacz and Robert Wilson (2007), "The 700 MHz Spectrum Auction: An Opportunity to Protect Competition In a Consolidating Industry" submitted to the U.S. Department of Justice, Antitrust Division.

Day, Robert and Peter Cramton (2008), "The Quadratic Core-Selecting Payment Rule for Combinatorial Auctions," Working Paper, University of Maryland.

Day, Robert and Paul Milgrom (2008), "Core-selecting Package Auctions," *International Journal of Game Theory*, 36, 393–407.

Day, Robert W. and S. Raghavan (2007), "Fair Payments for Efficient Allocations in Public Sector Combinatorial Auctions," *Management Science*, 53, 1389–1406.

Federal Communications Commission (2002), "Spectrum Policy Task Force," ET Docket No. 02-135.

Harsha, Pavithra, Cynthia Barnhart, David C. Parkes, Haoqi Zhang (2009), "Strong Activity Rules for Iterative Combinatorial Auctions," *Management Science*, forthcoming.

Klemperer, Paul (2004), *Auctions: Theory and Practice*, Princeton University Press.

Kwasnica, Anthony M., John O. Ledyard, Dave Porter, and Christine DeMartini (2005), "A New and Improved Design for Multi-Object Iterative Auctions," *Management Science*, 51, 419–434.

McMillan, John (1994), "Selling Spectrum Rights," *Journal of Economic Perspectives*, 8, 145–162.

Milgrom, Paul (2004), *Putting Auction Theory to Work*, Cambridge: Cambridge University Press.

Milgrom, Paul (2007), "Package Auctions and Exchanges," *Econometrica*, 75, 935–966.

Milgrom, Paul (2009), "Simplified Mechanisms with Applications to Sponsored Search and Package Auctions," *Games and Economic Behavior*, forthcoming.

Pagnozzi, Marco (2007), "Should Speculators Be Welcomed in Auctions?" Working Paper, Universita di Napoli Federico II.

Parkes, David C. (2006), "Iterative Combinatorial Auctions," in Peter Cramton, Yoav Shoham, and Richard Steinberg (eds.), *Combinatorial Auctions*, Chapter 2, 41–78, MIT Press.

Porter, David, Stephen Rassenti, Anil Roopnarine, and Vernon Smith (2003), "Combinatorial Auction Design," *Preceedings of the National Academy of Sciences*, 100, 11153–11157.

Distributing the Digital Dividend

Stephan Korehnke

Peter Cramton talked about the last step in the allocation process. I would like to start a bit earlier and would therefore like to outline the Vodafone position on what the digital dividend is, how we want to use it, and what we would like to do with it.

Stefan Seifert also said something at the beginning about the size of the digital dividend. We think that the digital dividend has to be defined in a way that forces us to look at TV channels, which were previously distributed in an analogue way. Now that we are in the digital age, we think that in theory, 75 percent of the current broadcast spectrum range could be released for new purposes.

I say "in theory"; it's not that we claim 300 MHz of this TV spectrum, but we claim a fair share of it. And we think that we need national debates in the EU member states on how to allocate this digital dividend spectrum, which is a valuable public good.

Across Europe, these national debates either have to be started or they are already underway. I think in Germany we have a good process going with all players in that respect: the ministry, the regulator, but also the broadcasters and telecommunication operators.

I would like to talk a bit about which factors should be taken into account when we talk about the digital dividend in Germany. First of all, the physical characteristics:

I think it's commonly known that lower frequencies can reach further than higher frequencies. So bringing broadband services to people could be done in low frequency areas in a cost-efficient way, and this, we think, is a unique opportunity to cover especially rural areas that do not have broadband coverage at the moment.

Second, the economic perspective. When we look at the economic effects, it can be shown that gains of up to 165 billion euros will arise if the dividend spectrum is allocated efficiently. That would mean that at least something between one third and one fourth of the dividend spectrum should be allocated to mobile services. This is the result of a study we did together with other mobile operators and suppliers.

Last but not least, we should look at the public interest. We should be aware that the Internet is becoming more and more important as a way for citizens to access information. Access to broadband services and to the Internet is part of the public's right to freedom of information. Consequently, there is no longer any contradiction between broadcast and mobile broadband services because they both serve the goal of ensuring freedom of information, media pluralism, and cultural diversity.

Furthermore, as we understand it, mobile broadband is also becoming a new distribution path for broadcasting content because we do not want to be—and we cannot be—producers of content. We will rely on the content that is produced by broadcasters and others. For them, it will therefore be a new way of delivering their services to their customers who today have no access to broadband services, especially in rural areas.

It is also important to have a look at current consumer demands, especially those of young people. For them, the Internet is their main source of information, and Internet browsing happens to offer more choice than traditional TV.

In Germany, the penetration of terrestrial broadcast services is particularly limited; I know it is different in some other member states, but here the penetration rate is lower than 10 percent, so the question is, do we have to reserve a very valuable public good for a penetration rate of 10 percent of the customers?

That is why we ultimately believe that the consumer should be at the top of the list when we decide how we will allocate this valuable spectrum.

How should this spectrum be allocated according to Vodafone Germany?

We think that we need a nationwide allocation, and thus we are not interested in just covering the white spaces. We think that we need a contiguous spectrum and the allocation should be made as soon as possible. The question then is, how much spectrum do we need? We are perfectly aware that at the moment the debate is about 72 MHz, a spectrum range that has also been allocated by the WRC to mobile services.

But we think that in order to bring services with a higher bandwidth to the consumer, we need more than 72 MHz. If we think a bit ahead and consider how much bandwidth the customer would like to have in the future, today's DSL speed of 6 MBit could also be attractive to the customer on a long-term basis. In order to deliver that on a mobile infrastructure to the customer, we would need 160 MHz. That figure was arrived at by a working group that consists of German mobile and fixed network operators.

Which allocation procedure should apply? One principle that we follow is infrastructure competition. We believe in infrastructure competition and we think that this spectrum should also be used to promote infrastructure competition. So I echo what Peter Cramton said, which is that the auction is natural way to distribute the spectrum. It is the prevailing procedure according to German law and would guarantee that whoever values the spectrum most and will provide the customer with the most innovative services will get it.

Another important question to be answered is, how can we reconcile the idea of infrastructure competition with the fact that the spectrum we are discussing at the moment is rather limited? We believe that we should adopt an innovative concept here. We think that the spectrum should be pooled in the rural areas so that a certain minimum bandwidth could be guaranteed. In the areas where there are DSL services and where we do not have to guarantee a certain bandwidth politically because people can benefit from broadband services, we should rely on infrastructure competition. This would ensure that we have different spectrum holders who can build out their networks and can differentiate themselves from each other by means of different kinds of services and bandwidth offers.

The network operation in rural areas would not allow for a sustainable business case, so as I said, we are not interested in merely covering the white spaces. We would like an allocation on a nationwide basis so that we could make use of the frequencies in the rural areas but also outside the rural areas, i.e. urban and suburban areas.

So the 72 MHz we are discussing at the moment is, from our perspective, a first step to deliver mobile broadband services to rural areas. A data rate of effectively 6 megabits or more, which I mentioned before as a long-term perspective, will unfortunately be difficult to achieve with the given amount of spectrum. If we pool the spectrum when it comes to the 72 MHz, a data rate of effectively 2-3 MBit or a bit more would be feasible. So we think that in a second step, further spectrum has to be released beneath 900 MHz. Preparatory work on that on both the international level and the national level should therefore be started.

The debate in Germany has in the last weeks and months very much focused on the question of how telecommunication operators should cover rural areas. We have very often publically stated that we are willing to contribute to the political goal of bringing mobile broadband services to these regions. We are committed to that and I think politicians can rely on what we have said so far.

How can this commitment be safeguarded? We think that we should also rely on a new model. We could for example define certain rural areas by zip codes that have to be covered first. Consequently, we would roll out the network in these areas first and would then make use of the spectrum in urban areas afterwards. That could be discussed in several forums; for example, one could think about a round table between the Länder [states] and the federal state.

What are our conclusions? We think that the dividend spectrum offers the chance to supply innovative mobile broadband services especially, but not only, to rural areas. From our perspective, we need 160 MHz in the long-term. The 72 MHz which are currently being discussed are a first step and we are committed to helping to bring mobile broadband services to rural areas, if, of course, the conditions are set correctly by the regulator. To conclude, I think we should really make use of this unique opportunity we have at the moment in Germany as well as in Europe.

Collective Use of Spectrum: Economic and Technical Factors

Simon Forge

It is a pleasure and a privilege to be here before you today. I am not sure if I'm going to supply some solutions to some of the things we have been talking about so far, or instead raise lot of problems. Probably the last one. But then, it's more fun, isn't it?

Anyway, basically what I am going to present comes from some work we have been doing over the last five years in analyzing future needs to spectrum, and specifically for a presentation for the RSPG. What they wanted to look at was really the idea of something being termed in European Commission terms, the collective use of spectrum. That has a very specific meaning for them. And it is not a large idea of the collective use of spectrum. It refers very much to the concept of what in the USA is termed 'white spaces'. But I have taken it also to include the ideas of a commons and what that means in a much larger sense is how we can perhaps go forward in the future. And that is what I want to talk to you about today—those two particular areas, very much perhaps concentrating on the idea of white spaces. This covers how much we use the spectrum at the moment and also, what that could mean for Europe?

At the end of last year I didn't really have a Christmas because we were working on a draft report for the European Parliament on spectrum policy. What we put forward in that was a fairly advanced idea—and that is what we were asked to do—to look at how Europe might be using spectrum in the future. One of the things that we tried to examine was how radio might be used in the future in the most general sense.

I am amused by the term wireless, which includes infrared, visible light, ultrasonics etc. yet what we are really talking about in forums such as this is some kind of radio. We are not talking about those other kinds of signal propagation, we are talking very much about the radio spectrum. And the way in which we use it today has been concentrated on two major applications. The first, as we all know, is broadcast, since the 1920s. The second is mobile communications of all kinds. So what we have come up with are ways of sharing spectrum in very limited ways. What we are now putting forward now are for far more spectrum users than we have at the moment, sharing in the instrument scientific and medical bands and other specific frequencies, say around 800 MHz, for opening garage doors and a few other things for RFID etc.

So what we said was there is key gap here for Europe's future. With a progressive release of far greater unlicensed bands, we ought to be thinking much more creatively about how we could use the commons in spectrum. Much of this technology originates in military applications. For instance, CDMA comes out of US military research, some of which goes back to WW2. There has been a lot of work on various alternative approaches such as frequency hopping as a form of frequency sharing.

So what we were interested in is looking at new sharing approaches and how we could establish perhaps an unlicensed commons in Europe. This is what we put forward in our report. It was quite well perceived by the European Parliament and what I was even more surprised by was that it was well perceived by the Commission. The European Commission, whatever may one think about it, has in fact been quite supportive of these kinds of concepts—basically because at heart they have the good of Europe in general as their goal, especially in spectrum management.

What do we mean by collective? What are the demands and rewards that we might have? And how could we actually achieve that inside the EU if we go down this kind of path? It is a fairly new way to think about radio propagation. As noted much of these sharing ideas for spectrum really come from the military and if we look at recent directions such as cognitive radio, many of the companies that dabble in that are part of the military industrial complex around Washington D.C. or on the West Coast. And we see a great military interest both in the UK and the USA in various ways of hiding signals be it for radar, with chirp signals, or for communications. What we are interested in is—can we harness these developments in radio propagation for the future? And are there ways in which we could create a commons in which people can use these signals in new ways. But also are we in fact using our spectrum really efficiently and that is something I want to turn to in a second.

So what do we mean by collective? I think we can say we have got three sorts of models, the Exclusive Use models, with managed allocation, command and control. They have cede assignment authority to a central authority which chooses the users. Then secondly we have a market, something that we have been speaking a lot about here and also secondary markets all with a property owning model in which we give rights to someone. These are two modes of exclusive use of our spectrum.

Then we have the Sharing Models, very different and perhaps difficult to understand at first, especially for those who not been working on this for quite some time. It may take decades for all to accept that perhaps we can have overlapping signals in the future. So in the commons we are looking at pure unlicensed spectrum.

More generally, new approaches should somehow avoid the patent problems, which plague us in 3G mobile and will plague us again in 4G. Because there is a new 'interesting' vessel, which just hove to view on the patents horizon, OFDMA, which may be firing broadsides for the next few years, as we saw with the 3GPP patents. So if one is going for sharing model, a first priority is to understand what the patent pool problems may be.

If we go for a mixed or collective approach we have to state how can we actually have people simultaneously conversing, communicating, receiving in the same geographical area. And that includes sharing spectrum in the commons by overlap. But it also includes the white space model, or hole-filling, with a dynamic use of spectrum, in which we hop around, because we sniff who is already using it and who should be using it. And then we either borrow or steal or we pay a subletting fee for the use of that spectrum. But way to maximize the economic growth, we think, is very much towards the collective use of spectrum. We think of this spectrum is being very crowded. But in fact spectrum analysis graphs from OFCOM from the UK show that this is not so. Here we are looking at three areas, the classic ITU divisions for mobile radio of rural, suburban and dense urban. And what we tend to see is that in the use spectrum, the red areas of high usage is jolly small compared with the blue areas, which are low usage. And this pattern continues throughout the day.

So we have to say—is scarcity real? Is this an artificial effect? Are we creating scarcity for somebody to make money or to control a particular market? If we look at the USA we have the same story. We see that very little of the US-spectrum is in fact in use heavily at any one time. Consequently we have to question whether spectrum allocation is really be used efficiently. And so we need to see change in a concept of spectrum and its management. We have to question should it be an ownable asset or is it just intellectual construct? Kevin Werbach's paper[32] goes into this quite extensively. I would recommend you have a look at it, if you are interested in this concept.

Traditional spectrum management concepts are based on spectrum as a physical asset denominated by the frequencies. We may now say that that is an artificially constraining mechanism. The property model is really evoking the tragedy of the anti-commons—in that

[32] K. Werbach,(2004), Supercommons: Toward a Unified Theory of Wireless Communication, Texas Law Review Vol. 82:863.

this scarce resource is in fact quite underused because there are multiple owners who do not use it? And each owner is endowed with the right to exclude others.

Thus a better approach may be to draw on usage privileges that did not presuppose ownership. And the baseline is how you use spectrum. And are you allowed to use it? And are you using your service responsibly—but notice—not necessarily the spectrum itself. In other words there is a separation, a division between service provision and spectrum usage, far more than in the past. What we want to do is to try and refocus, away from considering the ether as a scarce resource. We already have this useful model in the IMS Band (instrument of medical and scientific) which is perhaps heavily overused at the moment.

Hence we really have two models currently. We have this hard ownership of management through the markets where we can 'own' licensed spectrum. Or else it is given to us by the Government, especially because we are a broadcaster perhaps and it is not licensed at the economic price. Or we have this very soft view of ownership, where we may borrow or sub-license a small space perhaps for a limited time. There is no single owner here.

And then we have a new strand that really arrived in the late 1990s resulting in some PhD research in 2000/2001, although interest has been there for longer. And what we have is the principle of cognitive radio based on the software radio concept. Here we understand the characteristics of the ambient spectrum we are transmitting into. We understand the radio environment fairly clearly and so select those frequencies which are unused, an approach which has grown up over the last decade.

When we start to look at the value of spectrum for the 3G auctions we see a strong contrast. Working for one of the major operators in the UK just after the 3G auctions, I had the wonderful task of being an IT director who had to put together all of the media applications. This was real convergence of a telco and a media operation. But what we saw was an enormous auction payment that sucked up all the money needed for the technology and roll-out. We were poverty stricken by the design of that auction. I've almost seen a fist fight between a gentleman from another operator and the regulator responsible for that auction.

Effectively we have had an authoritarian managed spectrum allocation in the past. This needs to be replaced as we go forward with auctions. I am sorry about this Peter Cramton, but the problem is that the government, represented by a national treasury, may be very thankful for the many billions which such auctions provide.

So what is the efficiency of usage and are there is various types of usage? We should ask which type of usage and management approach is best for each user, rather than who will have it all. We should also ask—what is the value of that spectrum chunk to the economy and also what is the social value of that spectrum? For whom is it destined? And I think we forget too often that really the spectrum is a public resource. The end user is you and me—the consumer. We should be considering maximisation of use of the spectrum, with the idea of pooling the resource, not confining it to one user.

We have just been working on that for one Asian government with two analyses of a spectrum band's value, by two different approaches to valuation. One was to consider the value of the spectrum slice to the national economy. We had already done that with our own specific method, for the EU Digital Dividend, on behalf of a large operator in this country. We tried to understand what is the power of the spectrum to generate GDP-growth and generate jobs and then how does GDP per head go up.

The second approach was to build a business model of a 3G operator, as the auction was for a 3G spectrum offering. We tried to understand how much a contender would be prepared to pay, looking at the geography of that country, looking at everything from call centres to marketing and so building a business model. This gave the commercial value of the spectrum. One should understand what somebody will be actually prepared to pay rather than just put the money on deposit in the bank.

So why do need a collective use of spectrum? What is the business case? What we want to do is to compare the value to the EU of a commons with that of a market based approach of licenses. And what we may tend to see is that we are going to have, compared to licensed, more innovative usages, in mobile, possibly in TV and radio, perhaps with fixed radio loop over some new sharing protocols, especially for broadband. If we look at the collective license use we may also see far more possible usages in fixed radio local loop.

Recently we have just been doing work for the OECD, looking at the family's ICT needs in 2030 and what would not just the consumer, but the family want in terms of its education, its healthcare, or care of the elderly, as we are a greying population in the EU . We are saying is that radio in the future is not going to be confined to just a mobile industry and the broadcasters. There are going to be far more demands on it, perhaps more socially justifiable usages and we have to look at innovation for those social purposes. Moreover with a collective use of spectrum we have enormous repricing impacts on existing services, mobile especially and so fixed line pricing, all moving down towards 'near zero tariffs' perhaps . And what we are going towards is this great nirvana—or perhaps you see it as hell if you are in an operator.

Near zero tariffs is a very big and interesting subject for stimulating economies. So if we compare the approaches to spectrum management we may say that actually we could have licenses, also a commons, and also have a mixed or collective approach of white spaces. There is room for everyone here, but what we have is what is termed in colloquial English, "horses for courses" or usages suited to purpose. There are certainly special conditions, for instance where we will guarantee that the emergency services always get through. Those first responders must have priority. Therefore the ideas of managed command and control could be used although we can imagine creative usages of the various options for must-use in emergency, so we may modulate that set of spectrum management conditions.

The question is how much job creation, how much economic stimulus might we obtain through the various approaches. Markets in spectrum have a place and we can see where they might go. What we are really interested in, is, how easy it is to get into a market with a new innovation that uses radio. That is the way in which we are going to stimulate the economy in the future. Because if we are going towards a knowledge based society, then we have to free up the use of radio much more to be able to do that. One national regulator, when I presented this earlier in the year said afterwards, that there has been no innovation ever in unlicensed bands, apart from Bluetooth and WiFi. I didn't like to reply directly with—"well perhaps that is because you will not release spectrum so you are unlikely to stimulate any innovation—and also you would lose those fees which your government wants".

A needs analysis is required, to look at what is the basis on which we may plan for using radio in new and different ways. Here we include care services, diverse industrial usages, retail or logistics, with needs that show the social benefit and quality of life enhancements. How do we actually use the spectrum is unclear as future uses may be evolving, only transient. One thing we may be sure of is that it is more than communicating; it is the ability to use radio in very new ways. So the value of the collective use of spectrum is something that we are still working on, it is a work in progress. We would expect GDP stimulation from radio-usage to enhance productivity. From earlier work we have seen that if you put mobile into a small company, and Europe is a region of small companies, at least 6% increased productivity results, spread over several years in making the whole of the company mobile. What we would expect to see is if we can drive down the price of doing that and we open up the access, that we can add an extra 0.1 to 0.2 percent to GDP per annum. One may say that is heavily optimistic, completely wrong. In studies on the digital dividend, we estimated that optimal use of the UHF spectrum taken from TV for mobile services would bring in something like 340 billion Euros extra for the EU aggregated over a decade to 2020. This has effects on job creation and GDP stimulation in the long term.

So we can see that a spectrum management regime of transparent overlap of multiple signals would be very useful. There is a growing demand for radio usage in ways in which we could use these more unlicensed bands, more sharing and we agree a balance, also on the current allocations. Now that last point is perhaps the most significant for many people in this room and that is very much an open question—if you did bring in this technology, what would it do to the existing market? Well, what is interesting is trying to understand, which of the technologies is available to us and how do they operate? What we have come to is to look not so much at an index of interference but at an index of transparency, trying to understand the degree of overlap that one could use. This is of interest in military circles at the moment. In other words we may ask where we would put each of the technologies that we have at the moment and how transparent they are, how 'unseeable' are they by other users? And this is the way I think future radio technologies should be looked at, with devices and protocols now being worked on, be it use of the interstitial white spaces, or near field, short range, which is really in my view is a cop out, just using very high frequencies some like 40 GHZ, 60 GHZ, where everything is absorbed by O2-bonds. I mean that is interesting and it is useful, it has its place in things like body area networks. We want to have very low range signals and we do not want anyone else to capture them, so it has its place. But there is so much more. I think really we should be interested in long range shared spectrum of the orders of many kilometres. That is what future sharing technology should aim at.

If we look at a strategy for usage where will we use each of these approaches in a controlled way, i.e. market based and shared co-existing in commons, we could say that it is evident where you may use each of these forms of spectrum allocation. Where we have safety of life, where or perhaps 'heritage bands' in the military and where we have a mandate for usage which we cannot obviate for some reason, obviously command and control rules—this might be for air traffic control, but even here there may be more creative approaches. Where we have high competition at a commercial level—where spectrum is seen as a scarce resource, and one has to respond to this as a political animal has to—then the national treasury may come in demand money. Many are saying this demand never occurs. I think it does. Commercial drives are for TV, radio broadcast, satellite and mobile, and this is where we could reduce the kinds of competition whereby spectrum is a way of controlling the market. Instead we are starting to think about new services, new major technology networks, novel radio technologies, concepts of ad hoc networks, mesh networking. We will also be using industrial, environmental and emergency sensor networks far more as the cost of these radio networks are coming down.

Those who will exploit the new spectrum freedoms will be new start ups and novel technologies. And what we probably will get is a strategy of combinations, and that for a region like Europe it would probably make sense to start thinking now about where we are going to put each of these types of allocation and what kind of functions would go with them.

Now there are enormous regulatory hurdles. The general implications for the EU and for national regulatory agencies are EU-wide spectrum management coordination. Guidelines will be needed, especially to reshape current licences, which may now have subletting clauses for instance. Then for public services we may need administered incentive pricing to get owners of large blocks of spectrum to relinquish some. We would expect to see that the regulator will have more of a monitoring role in radio technology, almost a form of policing with greater type testing laboratories, plus national interference monitoring continuously. A colleague has suggested unmanned aerial vehicles to constantly patrol looking for naughty things being done with the spectrum. We may expect also much more international participation and a global level of decisions. Regulators may have to intercede more with neighbourhood countries and understand what is going on with overlapping spectrum geographies. But gradually we would expect less regularity activity. This may not be welcome for regulators. There will be fewer auctions or lotteries for commercial licences and trading as we move to sharing spectrum. A more active regulatory role in deployment of radio technology is, I think, the key change for a regulator.

Thus spectrum management strategies could be quite different to that we have had a strategy for the last, whatever it is, a hundred and seven years, in which we forbade everything. We only permitted explicit exceptions. Now we have to think about a new regime, in which we allow anything to happen. But we forbid explicit cases—a completely different mindset. A regulator changes from being a controller and commander to being a coordinator and facilitator. The decision criteria on how to use spectrum goes away from interference and the vision of spectrum as a marketable property changes into it as a publicly owned commodity.

Well, to show my enormous confidence in this here I show a graph which many people have shot at me with, using various calibre weapons. We see a descent in command and control management, a rise in spectrum markets, but also a rise in unlicensed, and this area here in bold is the sublet spectrum going towards 2035.

We have had some developments very recently. Earlier in November, I think it was the 4th, the USA's FCC approved the use of white spaces devices. I think that is interesting as immediately it happened, some six days later announce Dell that they are going to do cards for laptop with integrated white space facilities for licensed spectrum. So we already see innovation coming in from market. Clearwire's CEO in a telephone conversation with analysts stated they are investigating the uses of white space spectrum, specifically for rural areas. Now I think that is something that all of the operators in Europe, especially those who are concerned with the digital divide (be they fixed or mobile) should be looking at. And the interesting thing is white space approaches could form an entry point, at low cost, for the fixed line operators to enter the broadband radio and mobile world. All kinds of things open up when starting to use white space, especially in rural areas. In the UK, Ofcom has given various details on the release of white spaces inside the digital dividend bands after the switch over, and show interest in geographical white spaces for particular transmitter areas as well the idea of white spaces in spectrum.

Part 3: Convergence & Innovation

Regulation, Deregulation, Investment

Iris Henseler-Unger

1. There is an intensive debate in Germany about regulation and investment. At its center stands the question: Is there a conflict between regulation and investment? The debate started with Deutsche Telekom's plan to invest in "Fiber to the Cabinet" (VDSL) and competitors' plans to invest in "Fiber to the Building". As the regulator is interested in static and dynamic efficiency, we are highly engaged in this debate and we are looking for concrete results to guide our decision.

2. First of all, we should keep in mind that regulation is only one of several framework conditions for investment. There are various other factors driving investments: Society's openness to technological developments and innovation and a positive economic environment, which includes tax policy, labor market policy, and financing conditions. Flagship projects, e.g. e-government, attractive content, Internet of Things or GreenIT, and the local support of municipalities must also be mentioned. Regulation itself has different aspects: the law, the action and interaction of the national regulator, the government, courts, and the European legal framework.

The starting point and the framework of regulatory decisions are based on economic and legal considerations. In a nutshell: Economic aspects that justify regulation are monopolistic bottlenecks. They lie mainly in the access networks. The last mile is only to a small extent replicable. Furthermore, we are facing market entry barriers as a result of economies of scale and scope. The legal framework is described by the EU-Relevant-Market-Recommendation and the European Directives on electronic communication networks. We make decisions in formal and transparent proceedings. Our pricing decisions are based on efficient operator costs, which are quite important to us.

The competitors are given the right to access the dominant infrastructure at a price that mimics competition—the efficient operator costs. The idea is not only to give them access to the network based on conditions that are consistent with static efficiency, but our decisions also aim to set incentives for efficient investment for the incumbent and the competitors. If the regulated price was lower than the efficient market price, there would be a reduced incentive to invest in this infrastructure, and if it was higher, there would be an excess incentive to invest. Our goal is not to achieve maximum investment, but is oriented towards the concept of efficiency. Especially critical is the price of the local loop, the last mile. It is very important for the competitor and incumbent. It is key for promoting both intramodal and intermodal competition.

3. The results show that the actual regulatory regime is successful. There have been a large number of market entrants (around 270 network operators providing voice service) and we are seeing extensive investment by competitors and Deutsche Telekom. In 2008 competitors invested more than the incumbent, 3.7 billion euros compared to 2.8 billion euros. Other indicators show that competition works. Let me give you some examples. In the core networks, we observe competition. Local loop regulation has given competitors the chance to collocate at around 3,400 main distribution frame sites. These 44 percent of the main distribution frames are mostly concentrated in big cities. Over 8 million rented local loops reflect infrastructure-based competition. Even the bottleneck character of the infrastructure is diminishing.

4. Does the success of competition result in deregulation? Yes, it does. The number of regulated markets is a good indicator. The EU Market recommendation as of last year consisted of 18 markets.

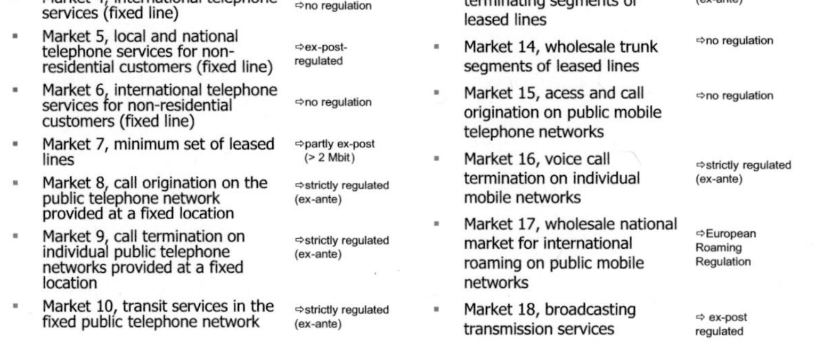

Figure 17: Markets Recommendation

Some of the markets have been strictly regulated, some ex-post regulated, some (e. g. international telephone services) have not been regulated at all, and some have only been partly regulated. Market 17 (international roaming) is not nationally regulated, but by the EU Commission.

In 2007 the number of markets contained in the recommendation was reduced from 18 to 7. Step by step, the German regulator will follow this reduction whenever possible; e.g. we will soon decide on a complete deregulation of the markets for telephone services for residential customers.

5. In this light of changing regulation and the reality of growing infrastructure-based competition, the political debate about regulation and investment is ongoing. A variety of opinions has been expressed. The starting point has been the investment in next generation networks, which means not only new capacity but also a new network structure, new technical possibilities, and new openness to convergence. Deutsche Telekom is calling for a reduction in regulation. It argues that regulation restricts its entrepreneurial freedom. The risk of investment in new markets should especially be reduced by means of an exemption of new (VDSL-) infrastructures from access regulation. That could give Deutsche Telekom a chance to earn a fair rate of return (pioneer profit). Competitors are demanding unhampered access to the monopoly infrastructure on fair terms and conditions as preconditions for their investment. They are demanding regulation and consistent prices (e.g. no price squeeze, no margin squeeze).

Which position—that of Deutsche Telekom or of its competitors—is proven by economic studies? One finds a confusing picture.

The answer to three main questions is crucial. We have seen this picture specifying 18 different markets, of which some are regulated, some are not regulated, and some are partly regulated. How can investment be related to a specific market, and when do we observe economies of scope? How do you measure regulatory action that is in fact so diversified? Does more investment mean more economic welfare?

Each of the different studies, of which Figure 18 shows only a selected overview, gives its own answer. How should we interpret their results?

Bundesnetzagentur

Regulatory Framework and Investment – Scientific Studies

Effects of regulation on investment have been subject of a number of different studies:

1. **London Economics and PWC (July 2006)**
2. **Waverman/Meschi/Reillier/Dasgupta (LeCG, September 2007)**
3. **Friederiszick/Grajek/Röller (ESMT, 2007)**
4. **Elixmann/Ilic/Neumann/Plückebaum (WIK Consult, 2008)**
5. **Czernich/Falck/Kießl/Kretschmer (ifo, 2008)**
6. **Möschel (2008)**
7. **Wey/Baake (DIW, 2008)**
8. **Cadman (SPC Network, 2007)**
9. **Gerpott (2006)**
10. **Blum/Growitsch/Krap (2007)**
11. **Heinacher/Preissl (2006)**

also others: McKinsey, Mercer/NERA, Arthur D. Little, Picot, Welfens, Haucap, Vogelsang ...

Figure 18: Regulatory Framework and Investment - Scientific Studies

Let me give you a first warning. Although financing issues and the quality of a study might not be related, it must always be critically asked, who ordered the study and who paid for it? The European Competitive Telecommunication Association (ECTA) financed studies 1 and 4. ETNO, the network of the incumbents, financed study 2. Deutsche Telekom financed studies 3, 7, and 11.

Let me give you a second warning: The complex technical, economic, and legal structure, which I tried to sketch in my introduction, demands some knowledge from the researcher. Some of the listed authors have deep knowledge of the sector, but others do not.

6. After these caveats, let me now present some studies: London Economics[33] analyzes investment in e-communication in EU member states and evaluates the determinants of investment. One of the main findings is that regulation does matter. There is a positive influence exerted by good regulation. What is important to me is that the study also proves that factors other than regulation have a more positive influence on a company's investment choices, e.g. the development on GDP. The study has "pros and cons". An important point is the way investment and regulation are quantified. The study underestimates the real

[33] London Economics (2006), An Assessment of the Regulatory Framework for Electronic Communications—Growth and Investment in the EU e-Communication Sector, Final Report to the European Commission.

amount of investment. It does not reflect all investments in the German market, because it concentrates only on some companies; small companies were not included in the study. The fact that Germany is among the countries with the lowest investment must therefore be questioned. In addition, the regulatory score card from ECTA monitoring the regulator's performance can be criticized. Catchwords in this respect are "double accounting", "mixture of activity", and "performance level".

7. Waverman et al.[34] focus on competition between cable and telco industries, i.e. inter-platform competition. The results are quite similar to those of Prof. Peitz. Regulation of local loops is regarded as very important. According to the study, the intensity of access regulation negatively affects investment in alternative and new access infrastructure. Intense regulation would reduce inter-platform competition. Minimizing access prices for local loops would promote intra-platform competition, but hamper investment in alternative infrastructures. Technically, Waverman has done better than the authors of the London Economics study. He concentrates on a rather basic economic decision, which helps to cope with basic effects. The study also includes new developments, such as investments in next generation networks. But a critique can also be formulated: The local loop price is not compared to efficient costs. Let me remind you that our price decision is oriented towards efficient costs in order to provide incentives for efficient investment. No price is chosen in order to maximize investment. Waverman's analysis focuses on inter-platform competition, which in Germany is quite unimportant. The reasons do not lie in telco regulation. The situation of inter-platform competition in European countries is quite divergent.

8. In the Röller et al. study[35] the relation between regulation and investment is addressed very generally. Investment and regulation are measured quite superficially. I like the result, which is that there is no significant effect of access regulation on the incumbent's investment in fixed line. That means that our regulation does not really influence the incumbent's behavior. But it does influence competitors' investments, especially those of entrants.

The study has some positive aspects. The authors attempted to avoid a simplistic approach, to distinguish between short- and long-term effects, and to use a dynamic specification. But there are problems too. Regulation is measured by an indicator developed by Plaut

[34] L. Waverman et al., (2007), Access Regulation and Infrastructure Investment in The Telecommunications Sector: An Empirical Investigation.

[35] L.-H. Röller et al., (2007), Analysing the Relationship Between Regulation and Investment in the Telecom Sector, ESMT Competition Analysis.

Economics, which is financed by Deutsche Telekom. It evaluates data and events from the perspective of an incumbent. Two examples: 1. The introduction of a newly regulated product—bitstream access—is valued negatively by Plaut. In contrast, it is valued positively on ECTA's scorecard. 2. To auction UMTS—spectrum is assessed negatively by Plaut, although it has given more spectrum to the market.

Investment data are taken from the Amadeus database. Amadeus does not consider investments by all German firms; especially those of smaller companies are lacking. Investment is therefore underestimated.

Röller et al. also do not reflect prices and efficient costs. They do not analyze the bottleneck character of the last mile. Without the possibility of renting the local loop, competitors' investment in core networks and technical equipment would not have taken place. Thus, local loop unbundling is the central precondition for infrastructure competition. Finally, Röller et al. do not consider new next generation networks.

9. Costs, profitability, market shares, and density of population are at the core of the WIK Consult study[36] published in September 2008. It analyzes whether there is a case for investing in Fiber to the Cabinet (VDSL) and Fiber to the Building. It concentrates on the business case for next generation access networks in Germany. There is a clear answer to the questions. If the incumbent is the first mover, it could cover about 75 percent with VDSL and 25 percent of households with Fiber to the Home (FTTH). A second VDSL infrastructure could be profitable for 18.5 percent of customers, while a second FTTH infrastructure would only be profitable for 0.3 percent.

WIK Consult promotes a strong regulator. It proposes a long list of regulatory measures. We should regulate access to fiber in addition to duct sharing (an obligation that is already in the market). We need bitstream access to these new infrastructures. We need transparency. The call for regulatory action culminates in the demand for a change in regulatory paradigm. Up to now we were engaged in providing fair access to an existing network. WIK proposes that regulators should now take part in defining the structure of future networks.

WIK's analyses are based on a solid quantification of the investment calculus. But the predicted consequences are too far-reaching and fundamental. Furthermore, WIK's conclusions are too pessimistic; my conclusion based on WIK's results is more positive. There will be investment in the new modern and private infrastructure in Germany, and in the case

[36] D. Elixmann et al., (2008), The Economics of Next Generation Access—Final Report.

of 75 percent of households, we have a chance to see a partial replication of the last mile in 18.5 percent of the cases for the first time. That is a big step forward in competition. Infrastructure competition is intensifying. We are already observing that in reality. But more fundamental: From my viewpoint, there is no reason for a shift in paradigm in regulation. Regulators need not and should not engage in the development of the structure of the network by means of direct regulatory action. We need an evolution of regulation, not a revolution.

10. Ifo[37] evaluates concrete network architecture. It clearly sees the importance of access to local loops in the process of liberalization. The unbundled local loop obligation—so Ifo—had its moment. That moment is over now. Local loop-based competition is not sustainable in the light of next generation networks. There will be no more market entry, no newcomers in the markets. There is no further need to regulate local loops.

The study concentrates on next generation networks, as WIK does. But its results are in sharp contrast to the others. Let me formulate a number of questions: If Deutsche Telekom shuts down main distribution frames today, what will the competitors who collocate at the main distribution frame to access the local loop unbundled do based on their own infrastructure investment? Remember: 3,400 main distribution frames are collocated by competitors. Will they have to cope with sunk costs? Can they finance additional investment in alternative local access? Will they have to de-invest and fall back on infrastructure-based competition? What will their business model be in the future? Can the regulator lean back and observe?

11. What lessons have we learned?

- Regression analysis is complicated, especially in terms of explaining investment, and it is even more complex when it comes to explaining sector investment. We all know.
- Regulation matters. Whether the reaction to regulation is evaluated positively or negatively is to a quite important extent preconditioned by the general point of view.
- Regulation should concentrate on non-replicable infrastructure. We should deregulate whenever possible to ensure efficient market information and decisions.

We would all agree that whenever there is regulation, it should provide a stable, transparent, and calculable framework for market players. It should enable new services, new market entries, and investment in networks. Efficient investment is of key importance.

---

[37] N. Czernich et al., (2008), Technologische Dynamik und Wettbewerbspotentiale, Ifo-Schnelldienst 19/2008.

The regulator is eager on the one hand to provide incentive for investment in NGN/NGA but on the other hand does not want to hamper the level of infrastructure competition reached up to now.

Key questions remain: What are efficient incentives for investment? No regulation? The studies show a diverging picture. Should there be regulatory holidays, as Deutsche Telekom demands? A risk premium on new infrastructure? A limitation on net neutrality? Promotion of cooperation? Promotion of separation of networks and services? How should we cope with a change of paradigm in network technology?

Let me complete the picture with my closing remarks and try out another answer to the question of how much regulation matters. A look at Deutsche Telekom's share prices shows that regulation has an influence, but compared to that of entrepreneurial decisions, not a huge one, as the following example shows: Our decision on the price of unbundled local loop price in 1999 meant 17 million euros less in sales volume for Deutsche Telekom. The engagement in Global One burnt through 450 million dollars in two years.